Footp

To Robert with very
best wishes.
Frederic (Gilly) Gilberthorpe

Footprints

One night I had a dream.

I dreamed I was walking along the beach with God and across the sky flashed scenes from my life. For each scene I noticed two sets of footprints in the sand, one belonged to me and the other to God. When the last scene of my life flashed before us I looked back at the footprints in the sand. I noticed that at times along the path of life there was only one set of footprints.

I also noticed that it happened at the very lowest and saddest times of my life. This really bothered me and I questioned God about it. 'God, You said that once I decided to follow You, You would walk with me all the way but I noticed that during the most troublesome time in my life there is only one set of footprints. I don't understand why in times when I needed You most, You would leave me.'

God replied, 'My precious, precious child, I love you and would never, never leave you during your times of trial and suffering. When you see only one set of footprints it was then that I carried you.'

Anon.

Footprints

Frederic Gilberthorpe

ISBN 0 9520505 0 1

Typeset and produced by Action Typesetting Limited, Gloucester
Cover illustration by J.W. Smith
Cover graphics by R. Thomas.
Printed and bound by the Cromwell Press, Broughton Gifford, Melksham

Dedication

This book is humbly dedicated to those who came back and in particular to the memory of those who didn't and to the wives, families and friends who waited often uncertainly for long periods of time for news of those of us caught up in the net.

My sincere thanks are extended to the International Red Cross for their unceasing efforts to maintain contact between warring factions irrespective of creed or nationality; to my friends in the New Zealand P.O.W. Association who so generously took the time and trouble to carry out research on my behalf and to Bill and Margaret Pedersen of Bulls, New Zealand for their unstinting support and friendship. My thanks also to Beryl Banks of Stone, Staffordshire for her helpful letters and photographs of her late husband 'Lofty' Banks, and finally to my wife, Mary, for her persistence and dedication in deciphering and typing my frequently unreadable manuscript.

Author's Note

Certain references, comments and observations made in connection with this account of my personal experiences were my genuine reactions to events and happenings current at that time and do not necessarily reflect my opinions as they stand today.

Contents

CHAPTER ONE

Anzio – Rome

In the bag

March in Italy can be a grim old month and possibly rates as the most forgettable month of the year because in March it isn't just the brass monkey conditions that prevail, for to cap it all – it rains.

The cold penetrated our already sodden clothing and the mud, absolute acres of it, created an additional problem inasmuch as it seeped and squelched in an almost obscene fashion, sucking at our protesting feet and spitefully managing, much to our general annoyance, to penetrate the gap between one's ankle and the top of the boot and thence to furtively ooze down the inside, mingling in a gleeful fashion with our sodden socks and frozen toes.

It was in that same winter of 1944, that the Allied Armies were frustratingly bogged down in a wide area north of Naples and south of Rome with the main point of contention being the entrenched positions held by the Germans on a line between Monte Cassino and the west coast of Italy. The situation there had reached an unacceptable stalemate as the Germans, commanding the heights of Monte Cassino, were able quite simply to exercise full control of the highway below, thus denying the Allies any hope of an advance that would result in the taking and liberating of Rome.

The only answer to this problem appeared to be in the considered landing of a large military force somewhere north of Cassino where it was hoped that an operation of this nature would be successful in relieving the pressure by drawing a part of the German army which was heavily committed in the defence of the main highway to Rome. This defensive line built by the Germans was known as the Gustav line and did in actual fact stretch across the entire width of Italy from Ortona on the Adriatic coast along a line roughly 40 miles north of Naples.

After much deliberation, a plan with the code name 'Shingle' was developed and that was how, on January 22nd, 1944 the operation for the landing 60 miles north of Naples took place on a beachhead of a small fishing port named Anzio, and on account of this, and as a very small cog in a very large wheel, I found myself in the mud of Anzio.

It was in early March that we finally surfaced in a partly wooded sector somewhere to the north west of the port of Anzio and overlooking the German positions scattered around an area known as the 'Factory': in actual fact this was a large agricultural settlement called Aprilia, built pre-war by order of Mussolini and destined for the use of peasants brought there to farm land recently reclaimed from the Pontine Marshes. From a distance it had the appearance of a fortress or a factory but it was an entirely self-supporting village enclosed within a huge brick wall but, situated as it was on the highest ground surrounding that area, it had now become the sole and, until recently, the uncontested property of the German 29th Panzer Grenadiers. This was, I believe, a situation which had been misjudged by the Allied Powers-that-be and on account of this area being so heavily fortified with a vast array of self propelled guns, tanks and infantry, a stalemate had arisen with neither side seeming anxious to exploit. Immediately to our left and bedded firmly and securely in a hull-down position was a German Tiger tank with a crew totally lacking in respect and uncaring enough to persist in scattering its shells around us. The muzzle velocity of this weapon was so great that on account of its close proximity to our position we noticed that what should have been the warning whine of the approaching shell was to be heard only after the shell had landed.

By day our position, exposed as it was, could scarcely be described as comfortable. Any incautious move would bring the wrath of the Tiger upon us and it was with some relief that we welcomed the hours of darkness. This darkness also brought with it a further blessing as it was to herald, on a nightly basis, the arrival of a fatigue party detailed to carry from whence we neither knew nor cared, a much welcomed hot meal and sometimes a supply of cigarettes and chocolate and very occasionally a letter from home.

Under cover of darkness, apart from the unavoidable hazard of stumbling along unlit paths, the element of personal danger to them was strictly negligible but, with an almost frenetic sense of urgency their burdens were rapidly dumped and the carrying party, absolved of all further commitment, would hastily retrace their steps towards base.

Dick Howarth, another Yorkshire lad from Mirfield, and I were responsible for radio communications which involved doing a two hours on and two hours off duty operated on a 24-hour cycle over an indeterminate period of time and which was a routine which demanded a tremendous amount of concentration. However, this problem had been well anticipated and on account of this we had each been allocated an assistant whose main function in life appeared to be keeping us awake. We existed in a tiny dug-out carved out of the side of a small hill and with sleeping space admittedly cramped but, for the use it got, perfectly adequate for our limited needs. Sleeping, waking and working all formed a part of a pattern difficult at times to actually relate to. Our immediate social circle in itself was limited. Sleeping and working alongside Dick produced, albeit subconsciously, an unspoken yet acceptable sense of mutual respect. He wasn't a great talker, I'd almost say introverted in his general outlook but still, should the situation arise, a firm, well-balanced friend. I'd only met him in Algiers during late December 1943 on my return from Egypt where I had completed a signals course and when I joined him in the H.Q. signals section.

Apart from him and our two helpers, we were fairly well isolated from the remainder of the squadron who were widely spread throughout the sector. Our duty broadly consisted of manning the radio set installed within the squadron H.Q. dug-out where we were blessed with the presence of the squadron leader, a Major Kay – a recent replacement and a person of whom I had little knowledge. The remaining occupant of our command post was our Squadron Sergeant Major Pat Beasley. Pat was a reservist called up at the beginning of the war and one who had a good name within the Regiment. He was a fair-minded chap, very likeable and a regular member of our football team, but apart from those mentioned, we saw very little of anyone else.

Dates, even at that time, meant very little to any of us, apart from remembering, on a daily basis, to change the number on the Kodex Camera which gave us a new coded sequence for use on the radio set. I do however remember the twelfth of March for two reasons, not the least being that the weather had taken a decided turn for the better. The sky turned on its charm presenting the brilliance of a true blue Italian miracle, but more importantly I remember that date chiefly on account of the day that was to follow.

We were warned to prepare for an action scheduled to take place during the early hours of the 13th and this order produced a hectic, frenetic need to ensure that all weapons were checked, cleaned and oiled, emergency rations were handed out and the Squadron for once assembled en masse after dark on that fateful Sunday night.

Dick and I had been allocated a new radio frequency on which to operate and our job was to keep abreast of the attacking group and to maintain maximum contact between our troops and to relay whatever information was passed to us back to Regimental H.Q.

We quietly formed up along a white taped start line with a series of whispered 'good luck' messages being exchanged between friends all keyed up to get on with whatever had to be done.

Silence at this stage was terribly important but seconds after a whispered command to move forward was given, all hell seemed to be let loose. Rapid firing Spandau machine guns notorious for their blistering rate of fire and for their deadly accuracy began spewing out their evil message from fixed firing positions bedded safely and securely within the German lines. Tracer bullets weaved gently in the dark night as though searching and seeking us out individually and threatening our impending destruction and, now that the Fritz seemed to have our range, we were soon subjected to an unwelcome spell of concentrated mortar fire.

Our 38 set, a radio backpack, heavy, clumsy and uncomfortable, was strapped to my back whilst Dick, by mutual agreement, laboriously carried out his private battle with the controls whilst at the same time trying to sift through a whole series of messages which were being transmitted. Many of the messages were totally incoherent with frequent cries for help, garbled messages, and an infuriating cacophony of confused crackling sounds all issuing forth from the radio, which seemed to turn the entire situation into an incomprehensible nightmare.

We still didn't know what our objective was but we somehow sensed that whatever was happening was not entirely in our favour. A series of shouted orders to the effect that we should halt and dig in didn't come as a total surprise as it became painfully obvious that whatever we had set out to do had simply not come about.

Time, they say, is relevant to a given situation and for my money, I'll go along with those sentiments. To us it seemed that we had been pressing forward for hours, yet, in retrospect, it was probably no more than perhaps 45 minutes. We appeared to have covered a considerable distance but again, on reflection, possibly no more than half a mile – if that! Dick, ruefully shaking his head, yelled out to me that so far, all the messages picked up on our 38 set had absolutely no value whatsoever. Several frantic calls for information were still coming over the air and I remember one rather peculiar message repeated over and over again in a high pitched hysterical voice informing the whole world, if for that matter anyone cared, that his, 'Sunray' – the agreed code word for the Commanding Officer – was dead. 'Marvellous,' we thought. 'Let's dig the bloody trench.'

Without doubt the Fritz had taken the initiative from us and we, of necessity, became industriously committed to belabouring the stubborn unyielding earth with our woefully inadequate entrenching tool which, for want of a more accurate description, could be likened to a child's seaside spade.

By first light and despite a persistent degree of animosity still being shown by the enemy, we had succeeded in digging through about three feet of earth on our frantic journey downwards towards Australia, whilst all around us could be heard the grunting, wheezing and cursing of troubled souls hell bent on a similar mission of great urgency. The long night was almost at an end, the early dawn had transformed itself into a heavily mist-enshrouded morning and, as though to herald the arrival of this uncertain day, the clamorous noise of conflict, such a short time ago so overpoweringly raucous, had gradually diminished to a mere whisper when suddenly, and completely unexpectedly, we were aghast to observe, emerging through the mist, a group of British Tommies. Unnoticed, at first sight, was the strange fact that they were completely unarmed although we were very soon to learn the reason why.

The Germans had already taken these chaps prisoner and were, with an alarming degree of Kraut craftiness, using them as a screen and now, having taken us by surprise, they commenced to sweep the area with several sharp bursts of fire. It never ceases to amaze me how certain incidents tend to imprint an indelible impression on one's mind and even today I recall a lasting memory of that incident which brings to mind a thought as to the shabby condition of their uniforms and the visual fact that they appeared to be just as weary as we ourselves were. It seemed that the enemy, incorrectly thinking that they had settled in full their account with us, turned round and with a series of orders levelled at the reluctant Engländers, and to the accompaniment of a severe bout of prodding with the sharp end of their weapons, they again slowly moved backwards into the swirling, damp early morning mist.

To our profound surprise, and to this very day I cannot admit to knowing who he was or from whence he came, we were startled by a khaki-clad figure leaping and clawing his way into our already over-occupied slit trench. We slowly rumbled from his pinky-white face and a single pip on his uniform that he was most likely a recent replacement, a brand spanking new second lieutenant unknown to us and apparently hell bent on seeking death or glory (preferably, I should imagine, in the reverse order) as, standing upright with his Colt 45, he blazed away at the now almost invisible group of Jerries wending their way backwards with their recently captured prisoners. Not to be outdone or, worse still, ignored by the retreating disinterested foe, his rapid, haphazard fire became orchestrated with a highly-pitched exhortation repeated over and over again inviting this lately victorious and happy band of Nazi pilgrims to 'Hande Hoch'.

Fortunately for us, the Jerry took absolutely no notice of our new-found friend and we found ourselves left isolated and surrounded only by the spooky, unnatural, overbearing silence of this strange morning. However, our youthful guest, now recovering from the gross indignity of being ignored by the very same people he had so recently set sail from England to confront, immediately began to assert his limited authority on us. The thought, it transpired, uppermost in our minds was to seek a safer, less exposed position than that in which we were now placed and Dick, eyes roving the area, was quick to indicate what appeared to be a fairly wide ditch only a matter of yards away from where we were and densely overgrown with a number of small trees, thick bushes and long grass.

An agreement, reluctantly accepted, and then only after much deliberation, involved the young officer moving back in the general direction of our own lines whilst we stayed hidden in the security of the ditch to await his eventual return. In retrospect, I must say that this was an ill-conceived decision why on earth did we not all three make our way backwards towards our own lines? I can only assume that his maxim was to the effect that any decision is better than indecision.

Dick and I sat and waited, hidden by the deep undergrowth that blanketed this part of the ditch which we had settled in. We sat and pondered on our situation. Movement, we decided, should be kept down to an absolute minimum as we could hear the Germans, who had once more resumed their sweep of the area, thrashing about in the undergrowth close by and calling out to each other as their search for stragglers continued. We both noticed, and admitted to, the deflated mood that had settled upon us over the past hour or so. No longer, it seemed, were we stimulated by the excess of adrenalin which, much earlier, had coursed so urgently through our nervous systems.

Now, however, we both felt absolutely drained of all energy and thought and, allowing for this reaction, our movements over the following crucial stage might well be better understood. We had remained in this position for what to us seemed an interminable period of time and we became increasingly frustrated by the continued absence of this chap who had, so far as we could see, failed in his promise to return. I don't suppose we were completely within our rights taking this negative attitude towards him but still, with these thoughts uppermost in our minds, we promptly came to the conclusion that our future prospects might best be served through our own efforts. For a while now no further sound of voices or indeed movement had been heard and we opted to leave the security which the well-shrouded bottom of the ditch had thoughtfully provided and began cautiously to clamber up to the top of the ditch where we would be better placed to take stock of the surrounding area.

It seemed to us completely unnecessary to take our belongings with us to the top of the ditch. We had several times tried to make contact through the radio, but as the frequency was changed on a daily basis, we had no knowledge of the new frequency and even though we had ranged throughout a complete cycle we had regrettably been unable to solicit any response. The overall height of the ditch from top to bottom couldn't have been more than a matter of perhaps twelve to fifteen feet and we had absolutely no hesitation in temporarily leaving our weapons, packs and radio at the bottom.

Being down at the bottom, well screened from prying eyes was a great advantage, but to offset that was the unacceptably cold and dank atmosphere which still pervaded the lower depths. Yet in our new found perch along the bank, the early morning sun was already desperately trying with its gradual, life-giving warmth to put the world to rights. Our stiffened joints revelled in this mild, comfortable, benevolent spell of luxury and I suppose it would be a fair admission to confess that following on the events leading up to our present situation we allowed ourselves to be foolishly lulled into a false sense of security mercifully oblivious of what was to follow.

Dick stretched out alongside me having slowly settled himself down on my left. We again heard a fair amount of activity which seemed to be going on all around us and even though it was still only early morning, we decided that it would be sensible to wait until dusk before starting out on our return towards our own lines. We must have talked quite a lot, I know we both dozed off a little, until finally we simultaneously became aware of a raging thirst. We were still stretched out languidly enjoying our new-found freedom, blissfully confident of our chances of reaching safety and hopefully downing a hot mug of tea. The thought of tea immediately brought us back to earth with the thought of our water bottles with their contents already depleted due to the demands of the previous night, lying at the bottom of the ditch. Dick jokingly pulled rank − he was a corporal − and demanded that I should be the one to climb down and retrieve our bottles.

Somehow I suspect we had been inactive for far too long and I'm sure that this was all being staged as an excuse to break the monotony and so I gladly accepted the diversion offered and sluggishly made my way down to where our equipment lay. I shouldn't imagine that I was away above a couple of minutes or so − it was, after all, only a matter of half-sliding, half-walking to the bottom, collecting our bottles and then clambering back up again. Dick had stood up simply to have a good stretch and stimulate circulation. There was a comfortable space between Dick and a heavily overgrown bush to the left of him and completely unaware of the imminent danger so soon to result in tragedy, I moved in to rejoin him on his left hand side.

He casually reached out his hand and took the proffered bottle from my grasp and, in a frozen moment of time, I remember so very vividly Dick lifting the uncorked bottle to his lips when suddenly and completely without warning two Jerries, schmeisers cocked and firmly held with the butt clasped at the waist, burst from behind the bush screening my left. An ear-splitting burst of fire scythed its way fractionally in front of me and by some strange quirk of circumstance completely spared me and yet it was so brutally accurate at a distance no greater than six feet to savagely cut down Dick. For a moment he stood with a look of total bewilderment on his face before spiralling, almost, I would say, in slow motion until he finally came to rest at my feet lying in a crumpled, scarcely moving tragic bundle of humanity.

It was only after this that I slowly began to realise my own predicament but on that score I had no need to fear. The Jerries, both of whom were now standing slightly apologetically and transfixed following the shooting of an unarmed man were now beginning to focus a little more attention in my direction as, looking down the muzzle of two sub-machine guns, I indicated that I would like to kneel down to see what could, if anything, be done to help Dick. The taller one of the two gave a brief nod and, taking this as an act of agreement, I knelt down over my friend. It was, however, all too painfully obvious that Dick was beyond human help and I tried to explain as best I could that I would like to reach into his pockets so as to remove his personal belongings. But whether they suspected a trick, or perhaps were anxious to return to their position, I do not know. I was rudely ordered to get to my feet and, standing before them with both arms raised above my head, I was scarcely aware that, whilst one of the two Germans kept me covered with his weapon, his mate began to conduct a very thorough search of my body whilst at the same time stripping my pockets of their contents and letting them fall to the ground.

In an awful detached way, I was already beginning to experience a strong feeling of uncontrollable guilt prompted by the thought that the body lying only a matter of inches

away from where I stood should belong to Dick and not me.
I was again to feel guilt on being very generously handed
back all the personal items that had been removed from my
pockets. Even my cigarettes were returned untouched yet we,
on so many occasions past, had stripped captured Germans
of everything removable, even down to the taking of a few
pathetic family photographs – useless, of course, to us, but
most likely treasured possessions in the eyes of their rightful
owners.

The three of us were moving back towards the German
lines and at that stage I had thankfully no knowledge of
what problems and hardships were to lie ahead and of the
immense distance which I would have to cover before finally
returning home. After an uncomfortable march lasting perhaps
half an hour or so, I wasn't altogether surprised to be dumped
into what had the appearance of a collection area. A little
while later, perhaps a hundred or so more prisoners were
unceremoniously formed up and slowly led away northwards
along a secondary road which would, we thought, eventually
take us towards Rome.

After only a very short distance along the dusty, uneven and
uncomfortably exposed road with a distinct scarcity of shrubs,
bushes and trees, we became the subject of an artillery barrage,
courtesy, I hasten to add, of our own people. Reason has it,
although we were unable to take advantage of it, that an
artillery spotter positioned somewhere within our own lines
had observed the straggling movement of a khaki-clad group
of prisoners being led away by a posse of field grey-clad
gentlemen belonging to the Third Reich. The barrage, heavy,
accurate and concentrated was being laid down on either side
and yet a reasonable distance from the road itself. In retrospect
it is my firm belief that this barrage was laid down to confuse
the enemy, thus offering us a chance to escape. There was,
however, no cover available in which to hide and anyhow long
before the mind started to function, we were urged on, at the
double, until we reached what Jerry decided was safe ground.

The weather had taken a decided turn for the better and
by late morning we had the makings of what promised to
be a moderately warm sunny day and, labouring with an
anti-climax following on the events of the past few hours,
we began to realise how very hungry and thirsty we were.
Somewhere, deep inside us, we slowly came to the conclusion

that for the rest of the war anyway, a new questionable phase in all our lives was beginning to take shape.

As time went by, tanks, transporters, supply vehicles and several large formations of ordinary infantry sweated and complained as they passed by laden down with their backpacks, weapons and so forth. At first we were simply pushed aside by the approaching tide of unfriendly Fritzes and very quickly our escorts began to realise the futility of the uneven struggle to keep us moving up the road and for this reason we were shunted, or relegated, call it what you may, to a route running parallel with the road and yet a fair distance away from it.

Walking along the road as we had been, was I suppose, comparatively easy as opposed to the less comfortable task which now faced us which involved picking our way over or around clusters of boulders, skirting like a plague small isolated bands of Jerries, most of whom were either scarcely out of their teens or alternatively bordering on the fringe of advanced dotage. These were the ones to watch for, young and cocky or elderly and nasty and they were all too willing to either take the mickey or direct abuse at us. They were in fact what we were to know as rear echelon troops, most of whom, in temperament, were oceans apart from their front line kameraden. Ditches we found to be yet another obstacle as, with the recent spells of heavy rain, they were uncomfortably full and one either jumped across or fell in, the choice was there for the taking. On top of all this, we had a ravenous horde of midges and mosquitoes to contend with plus the odd, almost casual attention of several American Mustangs which, swooping low and completely unchallenged, raked the area, generously scattering their load 'twixt friend and foe.

The thought of taking a long cool drink of water was rapidly becoming obsessional and several of us had begun to complain vociferously to the guards who, although having so far behaved quite decently, were insistent in their response that they were at that moment in time either unable or unwilling to oblige. We must have covered at least twelve miles or so and the pace, lack of sleep and shortage of water were beginning to have an effect on us. One of the Jerries, fluent in a dozen words of English, gave us to understand that our immediate destination was Rome. Darkness, however, began to overtake us and the Eternal City we gathered was too far distant to be reached in the time remaining. From the German point of view it would be unwise for them to continue the march and attempt to control us once darkness had set in. A frantic search was well under way to find a holding area suitable for our temporary confinement and before long, one of the Jerries sent ahead returned to the main party with a look of relief on his face. He had, it transpired, located a small farm which we discovered possibly a mile or so to the west of the road and which on account of its close proximity to the fighting had been abandoned. Judging by its appearance it had never produced much above a low level of existence and amongst several wooden outbuildings and the unhappy-looking farmhouse now almost completely demolished, stood a large, fairly modern and substantial brick storehouse with a floor luxuriously carpeted with a liberal scattering of straw and this, we gathered, was to be representative of our first night's accommodation as guests of the Third Reich.

We could, I suppose, have done worse. The guards, ever watchful, firm, but correct, had quickly organised a supply of drinking water courtesy of a decrepit, creaking but thankfully serviceable iron pump and, to crown this munificent bounty we were to have meat. A stray, very elderly and infirm sheep had somewhat regrettably (for the sheep) attracted the attention of one of our younger captors and he, encouraged by the blandishments of his colleagues, approached the animal from behind, levelled his rifle and very quickly, from very close quarters, shot off its head.

Our 'few words of English speaking Jerry' came over and ordered us into the storehouse calling and miming for a volunteer with however little butchering expertise to come forward to skin and cut up the bloody carcass. It was, I was told, a messy job. Who the 'butcher' was doesn't really matter — I've long since forgotten what he looked like — he was never a butcher in the true sense of the word. He was, I remember, taken under guard to what little was left of the farmhouse kitchen and there he did labour upon the poor old sheep which was finally laid to rest in a huge metal boiler suitably wreathed midst a succulent mound of recently liberated jacket potatoes, the whole of which was soon bubbling away merrily over a lighted wood fire.

Goodness only knows how long it took before it was finally declared tender enough for our happy band of philistines to devour, but I can unconditionally testify that never before nor since have I tasted a finer, more succulent meal than that provided albeit unknowingly by some unwitting Italian farmer last seen, no doubt, legging it up the Appian Way. However, joking aside, little did we then realise that this meal was to become far more memorable than we were likely to suspect. In fact, I would go so far as to say that, without question, this meal was to be our best for so long as hostilities lasted. That meal and the events leading up to it should, I suppose, have helped to create some kind of bond between we prisoners but possibly due to circumstance, fatigue, guilt or I know not what, there was a strange oppressive feeling of isolation which seemed at times to smother any attempt at conversation. For a short period of time the welcome drink of water, the satisfying meat stew and the night's rest seemed to a certain extent to alleviate some of the stress that had built up within us, but in a way it was, I suppose, what the pain barrier is to an athlete. We didn't know it then but we had a lot of barriers in front of us which would in time be overcome but our number one barrier, although at that time we were totally lacking the awareness of it, was the dire need to accept the situation that we were now in and hopefully meet and face whatever problems were to lie ahead.

We were up, stiff, but thankfully refreshed after a cold semi-wakeful night, relieved in some strange way to be moving even though it was in the wrong direction. I'd tossed and turned so many times during that long night; I'd pondered on the future, looked back on things past. I'd wondered if someone would stumble across where I had left Dick and perhaps make sure he got a decent burial. I had thoughts of home. I had heard the guards calling out to each other and the odd rattle as they checked the metal bar which secured the door from the outside. There had been the long dull intermittent rumble of heavy artillery shells landing, on which side it was impossible to guess. The odd plane could be heard now and again, engines churning as the machine, most likely heavily laden with a batch of bombs, possibly anti-personnel – butterfly bombs we called them – deadly in their application and highly acclaimed by the Kraut for their nuisance value. All in all it hadn't been a terribly good night but at least, thankfully, it was over.

We were soon on the march once more. Jerry was happy, he'd successfully counted out the correct number of captive bodies, and the early morning sun had shown itself, and was in fact producing at the very moment we commenced our journey a distant view of unprecedented beauty, the dome of St. Peter's bathed in the golden light of this early sunrise. I clearly recollect this glorious, breathtaking spectacle which instilled very deeply within us all I feel sure, a positive unrestrained promise of hope in this most uncertain future.

One would have thought that all troop movements would be carried out under cover of darkness but this wasn't to be the case. The road, fairly narrow I must admit, was again heavily congested with troops, trucks and so forth. We plodded on as before, off the highway, grateful for the infrequent rests, warily skirting the detachments of troops although sometimes contact was unavoidable and there were predictably the odd spontaneous clashes with the more bellicose members of the Hun tribe. Credit, however, must again be given to our escort who, generally speaking, did their utmost to prevent these head-to-head confrontations.

It had been a warm day, there had been moments of extra exertion and now having progressed to mid-afternoon with no sign of a refreshing sip of water, our pace had been drastically reduced as one would expect. In captivity, we were not slow to realise that our priority rating had somehow reached an all-time low. No drinks, no food, get up, sit up, sit down, shut up, we were certainly on the fringe of a drastic meaningful bout of re-education. Already we were picking up new words. Raus meant get up, schnell – quick, pause – rest and so forth.

By early afternoon, tired and dispirited, we made our final approach towards the outskirts of Rome. The area was still fairly countrified and it was here that we came across a series of huge, I thought, hangar-like buildings covering several acres of ground and protected by high mesh fencing. Most of these buildings appeared to be deserted but around the next corner we came across a rather imposing entrance. It was a huge garish archway with two words, 'Cine Citta', boldly emblazoned across the top of the frame. A sentry box stood either side of the solid gate which had been pushed open to allow us inside. Once inside it became painfully obvious that we were now the latest batch of inmates in a very temporary prison camp. These basic camps were known as Dulags or to give them their full title, Durchgangslagers – transit camps – although to say 'basic' was possibly an overstatement. We were accosted on all sides by a host of grubby, unshaven, unwashed and hungry-looking inmates. There were Yanks, Aussies, Poms (of course) and even a few Ities, Greeks and Indians thrown in for good measure. It was a bewildering hotchpotch of seething restless humanity, most of whom seemed to be engaged in calling out advice, questions or scrounging for cigarettes – which we hadn't got anyway; what few we had had at the beginning had by this time been used – and most of all we had the whingers repeating over and over again their dire warnings mainly concerning the depressing state of facilities within this camp.

Apart from a ridiculously high number of roll-calls – Jerry always went over the top on roll-calls – and the badly organised hand-out of bread, soup and ersatz tea, we were left very much to our own devices. All prisoners it seems were housed in one huge cavern-like studio. Yes, we were correct in our assumption – we had somehow thought that with a name like Cine Citta over the main gate and these huge buildings within what else could it be? But here was no Clark Gable to win the war for us and Betty Grable could scarcely be expected to be found lurking in these bleak studios so it was just down to us, a motley mixed-up shabby bunch of prisoners called in to play the bit part of a crowd of unfed, unpaid and unwanted extras.

Washing and toilet facilities were at a premium and the inside of the studio which was to provide us with a modicum of shelter proved to be a most inhospitable hole, draughty, devoid of heat and lacking even a minimal degree of comfort. A thin layer of straw was laid unevenly over the floor and with the stench of urine and other bodily odours pervading the dank fetid air from its over usage, the thought of actually lying on it minus any other covering to protect against the cold night air was a consummation not very devoutly to be wished. Several of us, intent on seeking a more acceptable standard of existence, were already scavenging, so far as one was able to see, the interior of this black hole of Calcutta when suddenly, hearing what sounded like shrieks of delight emanating from the far left hand corner of the studio, we hastened over to find a bunch of Kriegies apparently hell bent on tearing the wall down. Slowly, the motive behind this mindless act of vandalism became clear. This, it had been realised, was a soundproof film studio and having pushed our way to the front we very quickly discovered on running our fingers along the damaged wall that the inner portion consisted of huge layers of fibreglass sheeting. What a burden to be young and stupid! We gleefully carted back several of these sheets which were quickly converted into makeshift beds and later still, hour after hour throughout that long night, we tossed and turned, irritated beyond belief by what we wrongly suspected to be fleas, lice or some similar pest. However, in the cold light of dawn and through the expressed wisdom of some bespectacled, latter-day Cassandra, we learned to our cost that our lack of rest and the numerous small irritating cuts covering the whole of our bodies were actually caused by the minutely-woven glass fibres with which we had foolishly made our beds.

We were soon up and about prompted by that repetitive, ever-endearing and warm-hearted invitation that all Krauts with a mouth — and that means all of them — drooled over, it must have been a re-awakened lust for power. 'Raus!' they called. 'Schnell!' 'Raus!' 'Appell!' Why couldn't these ignorant toads simply say 'Will you please come out and be counted?' Anyhow, why bother? — they couldn't count. For the sake of simplicity we stood in rows of five, the digits of one hand raised by all guards present just to indicate 5, and then the pushing would begin. Eventually lined up we were counted and re-counted, checked and double-checked. Here, it seemed, we had a master race of Teutonic heroes who couldn't add up.

Our what you might call, first official introduction to this wartime version of Mastermind was a foretaste of this devilishly-devised system which was to constantly dog our paths for a long time to come. It has been jokingly said that the Germans said, 'Ve haf ways to make you talk'. If, indeed, that was correct, then why the hell had they not found ways to make them count? Jerry may have been a good soldier, an important cog in an efficient fighting machine but, by God, in every other respect he was as thick as a bag!

Now I haven't mentioned this, although at the time it was terribly important, but we had on the previous day missed out on all food — we'd arrived too late and that day's banquet had already been well and truly disposed of and so it came to pass that with ravenous anticipation we eagerly awaited the bread and soup ration scheduled to appear at mid-day. Appear it did. Dead on the stroke of twelve, or so it was said, ceremoniously carried in, not with a flourish, but with a reverence almost akin to that shown to a highly venerated relic devoutly exhibited by the church on an important feast day.

The less fastidious amongst us were well to the front of this noisy queue. Hunger was compelling me and the others who, like myself, had not eaten since the night before last, but one look at this ghastly, revolting brew was enough to upset, for the present time anyhow, the most hardy, indelicate stomach. It was not a pretty sight, a huge pail of greyish-green matter with the odd turgid leaf of well-rotted cabbage struggling on the surface to survive, and complemented, for want of a better word, with a meagre quantity of barley. Hungry as I was, it seemed more than likely to be quite a while before my palate would become sufficiently attuned to cope with such awful rubbish. On the fringe of this crowd stood a lurking Oliver Twist-type character, his face pinched with hunger, already beseeching me with one outstretched hand reaching out for the tin bowl containing my measly ration of this foul concoction, begging to be allowed to drink it rather than see it wasted. He gloomily predicted that before long I'd be only too grateful to accept this rubbish and in the fullness of time learn to enjoy it. I laughed but believe me his prediction was to prove alarmingly correct.

The good news was that an issue of a 1.5 kilogram loaf, to be shared between each group of 15 men, was up for grabs. The bad news was, that to equally divide such a loaf into fifteen identical portions using nothing other than a piece of crudely sharpened metal not only required the steady hand of a skilled surgeon but one imbued with the wisdom and judgement of Solomon.

This, to a well nourished over-weight critic may, with a lack of understanding, seem pretty childish but the fact is that the delivery and sharing of these loaves could set off a quarrel, create an enormous feeling of jealousy or perhaps bring a crafty smile to the face of one who may have judged himself lucky enough to get a slightly larger piece of the action.

Bread. The very word was, in the months to follow, destined to become obsessional. On many occasions it was the only topic of conversation certain to create a reaction. Even the Jerries were sometimes quite unwittingly drawn in on the subject. Should, for some reason, the bread issue be delayed we, who relied on it for sustenance, would gather near the supply centre and chant our silly little ditty which, I believe, went something like this.

> Fünfzehn mann ein brot,
> Fünfzehn mann ein brot,
> I eat, I eat, a lot
> Mein Gott!

The reaction by the Jerry after several tuneless but robust renditions of this jovial ditty inevitably produced a similar childlike result. They suspended the bread issue until long after order had been restored.

Cine Citta was a rough old camp whose facilities were, as I've already mentioned, very, very basic. There were, I should imagine, several hundred or so inmates sharing a communal trench for all our toilet needs. I can't quite remember whether there was one or perhaps two cold water taps plumbed in, maliciously, I thought, out of doors and so one can easily imagine that, with the likelihood of yet another cold, wet spell, there was no immediate rush to compete for the use of the washing trough.

One notable event took place during the afternoon of the following day when, standing a short distance from the main entrance to the camp, I was surprised to see the gate opened to admit a Catholic priest. He very quickly came amongst us and having asked us to gather around him, he explained that he was present as a representative of the Vatican with a mission to compile a list of our names and addresses which, he promised, would be read out over the Vatican Radio that very same evening and hopefully this broadcast would be picked up in England. We were, I must shamefully admit, very sceptical and indeed suspicious as to his true motive but on the other hand we could scarcely imagine a man of the cloth being involved in any skulduggery with the Hun so, without further ado, we each submitted our particulars. There was after all little to lose, and one could readily envisage the bald statement within the telegram sent out to one's next of kin which would simply read 'Missing in Action'. This information was broadcast as promised and was acted on just as it was intended although at that particular time I was unaware that my parents had been contacted. I did find out after the war that groups of volunteers scattered throughout our country devoted a considerable amount of their time to monitoring Vatican Radio broadcasts, collating information, mainly regarding P.O.W.s, and passing this news on by post to the next-of-kin. In my own case, this information was received and passed on to my parents by some unknown lady residing in Manchester.

It would, we knew, take a long time and, I suppose, a lot of bitter experience, before we would be able to accept our given lot. We did, not very gladly, but solely of necessity, come to terms with our situation chiefly by forming ourselves into small protective tribal units, but at this very early stage we stood apart, selfish, isolated and unashamedly paranoid and had this condition persisted as indeed in isolated cases it did, then it could simply and tragically develop into a self-destructive catastrophe.

It was only a short time since we were captured, possibly, although time didn't really matter, as short as seven or maybe eight days and yet already we had, what for want of a better word, one could perhaps best describe as phase one of a lengthy period of 'conditioning'. We'd started to eat the soup − it was exactly the same soup that only a matter of a week earlier we had unreservedly rejected and yet now, with one's stomach beginning to feel a wee bit neglected, we not only queued for our ration, we joined the tail-enders of the queue for what came to be known as 'spares' or 'seconds'. We were learning a great deal about the art of patience and accepting the fact that it was most unlikely that things would get any better. We didn't move about a lot − moving meant energy expended and a burning up of valuable calories. We sat outside if the sun shone and inside if it rained. Cleanliness belonged to the past and it soon came about that dirty bodies plus malnutrition equalled body lice.

If you've never had body lice − and I don't suppose for one moment that you have − then you've missed nothing but you just won't be able to understand the absolute torment brought about by these little perishers. They love body hair, in fact they revel in it, amongst it they are warm and comfortable, and with an unlimited number of bodies to feast off, they simply enjoyed life to the full and there they bred like the clappers. They irritate, debilitate and their numbers increase alarmingly by the hour. We were issued with the German kleider laus pulver, a rather grandiose title for a totally useless, 'clothing louse powder'. They bred under the outer layer of skin, kept

warm by the hair, or along the seams of our trousers and
shirts and we sat for hours trying either to pick them out of
our flesh or destroy them by running burning pieces of paper
along the seams of our clothing, hopefully settling for a 10%
success rate.

None of us quite appreciated that, although to us at any
rate, Rome existed only in our imaginations, we had unwillingly occupied a few sadly neglected acres of it for a short
period of time. Funny to think that everybody must have heard
about Nero being in Rome but I'll bet nobody remembers us.
That, however, is not quite true. Fritz hadn't forgotten us,
in fact he must have liked us because he sent along several
large trucks with a lot of Fritz soldiers. They said their
usual friendly sayings that friendly Germans like saying such
as Raus, Schnell, Einsteigen and Ruhe but the end product was
the same, 'Get up, shut up and get on these blasted trucks –
quick!' We were up and away so quickly we didn't even have
time to compliment the chef.

CHAPTER TWO

Latrina – Tuscany (Dulag 32)
Lice with everything

Setting off, clinging precariously to the steel upper structure supporting the canvas sheeting of the lorry, we were mildly curious to see what we could of the centre of Rome as we blasted our way with horns blaring, and the odd Italian foolish enough to step off a pavement without exercising due care would receive a torrent of Teutonic abuse from the guards perched on the back of the tailboard.

Tightly packed and with little or no room to sit, I was able to catch an occasional glimpse of this tantalizing and seemingly carefree city. Italians both young and old could be seen happily free of a war they said they never really wanted whilst we were being unceremoniously carted away to God knows where or for how long. One final glimpse of the Colosseum to our right, a smart left hand sweep and we were over the Tiber and again heading north.

The Jerry, considerate and splendidly generous as ever, had given each of us a piece of black bread and more out of boredom, I suppose, rather than from the sheer appreciation of this gourmet delight, we started to chew on this dry and very tasteless bread. Several hours later and long after the hour of darkness, we began to regret our reckless abandonment of common sense – we were thirsty, in fact we had a raging thirst. This bread, so dry, had now resulted in a dire need to quench our thirst.

Our convoy, again assuming a low priority, was frequently taken off the road in order to allow more important and urgent transport to take precedence. We became restless and aggravated by the constant delays, and our inability to relax due to our being packed so closely together prompted one voice to complain that he felt like 'a bloody sardine'. We demanded of our guards that a stop should be made for toilet purposes although the only answer received was a continual 'Bald' which we quickly discovered to mean 'Soon'. Soon, however, was a long way off before our stiff and cramped bodies were allowed to half fall off the truck for a quick al fresco toilet.

Getting back on the truck and having relieved ourselves, I could sense a slight relaxation of the tension that had been fractiously building up to almost uncontrollable proportions. We organised a rota system whereby a small percentage of us could sit for thirty minutes at the expense of the rest who would bunch up even more tightly to allow a fair period of rest for all.

The night finally ended in what could only be modestly described as a feat of endurance. We had ground to a halt so many times, we had taken detours over rough ground and, having covered a possible distance of 120–130 miles under these conditions, our relief could be imagined when, in the cold uncharitable light of a grey dawn, we were disembarked to line up alongside a mobile drinking water bowser where we each received a welcome drink of heavily chlorinated water. Following a series of excited yelps and screams from our German captors – they could never communicate in ordinary tones – we returned to the unwelcoming fetid atmosphere of the truck. Already in this short period of captivity we were subconsciously beginning to relate and to become absorbed within the system. New words, alien at first, were now becoming part of a new understanding. A few, dreary in their repetition throughout our stay, were notably and in order of usage: 'Es Gibts Kein' – 'there is nothing'; 'Raus' – 'get up'; 'Ruhe' – 'shut up' and a pair of similarly useless words 'Aussteigen' and 'Einsteigen' meaning to 'get off' and 'get on'. At this particular moment in our meaningful relationship with the Kraut we were in the middle of a frenzied bout of an 'einsteigen'! Journeying on and peering out through dust-blinkered eyes, it was pleasing to observe a marked decrease in the volume of traffic now using the road. Fairly obvious though when one comes to think of it, the Allied Air Forces were very much in command of the air, and with a policy of 'if it moves, hit it', there was little to be wondered at the meagre daylight movement of transport. We had now jerked our way around a series of detours controlled by a weary-looking detachment of German Feld Polizei – what a strange looking outfit they were clad in dingy field grey with their chamber pot-like steel helmets and sporting a huge metal badge of office across their chests suspended, it seemed by a neck chain. All signals were given by a semaphore-like action carried out by a series of movements with two sticks, one in each hand, with a large circular disc at the end of each. Picking our way carefully through an area recently devastated by, I should imagine, a series of air strikes, we came from time to time across bits and pieces of evidence which gave us the name of this town – it was Arezzo, a town of obvious importance with a series of roads which not only pointed north and south but were possibly capable of giving access to many other areas. In addition to its availability as a major road junction, we also noticed a very large railway junction which, judging by its devastated appearance, must have been the prime subject of the recent air-raids.

From that point onwards we became completely disorientated – not that it mattered a damn one way or the other. We left Arezzo and ground our way slowly along a secondary road and, after perhaps another hour or so driving across country, we arrived at our destination – Latrina.

Latrina, difficult to describe, sounds rather like an Italian word for 'toilet' and, as we were to discover during and after several particularly heavy bouts of rain, the camp took on the appearance of a badly-run toilet, except perhaps for the fact that the average toilet was more plush than this place.

It was raining when we arrived and having been summarily 'Aussteigened' – my word for it – and ushered unceremoniously through the main gate, I was able to take in the full beauty of the scene. Talk about the rich tapestries of life and here we had them all for the asking. The Germans didn't look pleased to have us, their dogs, the largest and meanest looking creatures I've ever seen, cast a lean and hungry look over each and every one of us as though mentally assessing who they took to be the tastiest morsel among us. Barking, whining and straining at the leash, these monsters were the living proof that Anglophobes existed indeed quite prolifically within the animal kingdom.

Our first steps inside the camp were accompanied by a muffled obscene squelching as our boots struggled to surface out of the mud. Hordes of prisoners assailed our ears with the customary but hopelessly inane questions mainly concerning rumours of a hopefully rapid approach of the liberating armies who, at that particular moment, were bogged down many miles distant from here. Had we got any cigarettes? Where did we come from? And countless other equally useless questions.

In answer to our questions we received a most discouraging response. It was, they said, a lousy camp, no heating, little food and judging by the hopeless and blank look on each face, we began to regret our arrival at Dulag 32.

On entering the main gate we got our first appreciation of its layout. In front of us gaped a large open square, positively oozing mud and, with a little imagination, and had the climate been a great deal more tropical, one could almost imagine a horde of crocodiles or alligators surfacing from its stygian depths. On our left, lined up in symmetrical fashion, were a number of large wooden barrack-type huts whilst over to the right stood a brick building which boasted a large smoky chimney – this, we already decided, was the mis-named cookhouse. Further along, and still to the right, was a small row of sturdily-built cubicles which, seeing them for the first time, reminded me of a similar type normally used in civvy street to house a dustbin or perhaps a few domestic tools. These, we were to learn, were the 'bunkers' and any observed deviation from the path of righteousness according to the Kraut's holy law would result in the offender spending a period of isolation in one of these tiny compartments.

Just beyond the bunkers we had the latrine trench. Now this trench, possibly 30 feet long and about 2 feet wide was considered sufficient to meet the needs of around one thousand prisoners. Balancing, squatting precariously on one's heels in this festering mud was no mean feat and, at peak times, the less acrobatic amongst us would too frequently be seen taking a backward dive into the filthy morass. This camp was not new and until recent times had most probably been an Italian camp but since September of the previous year when they had capitulated to the Allied Armies, these camps had been taken over by Jerry. A goon box perched high on timbered stilts stood at each corner, each box containing a non-descript but very alert guard complete with machine gun and searchlight. A double row of barbed wire fences approximately three feet or more apart completely encompassed the camp. Each fence, possibly ten feet high, represented a tantalizing gap between freedom and captivity. Inside the camp was yet another unappealing feature, the infamously named trip wire. This single strand of wire no more than a foot above the ground and spaced six feet or more from the high inner fence was placed there as a warning and anyone setting foot over the trip wire without prior permission would be shot.

In addition to the goons in their goon boxes, we had foot patrol guards constantly walking around the perimeter, guards at the main gate and an occasional guard snooping around the huts hoping to sniff out some real or non-existent crime. Looking back towards the main gate one got a remarkable view of the old village of Latrina perched high on a distant hill and looking down, it seemed, in complete and utter bewilderment at what was now happening to disturb its peace. The camp Man-Of-Confidence, in this case an American Top Sergeant, was waiting with his henchmen to allocate we new arrivals amongst the available barrack huts. I can only be guessing but I believe these huts capable perhaps of accommodating 30 or 40 souls would house somewhere between 60 to 80 prisoners. Wooden bunks, two tiers high, lined each side of the hut and the space between the two rows was taken up with a pair of rough plain wooden tables with matching benches to provide seating accommodation for possibly twenty or so of the inmates, with those unlucky enough to gain a perch having little or no choice but to lie on their bed. The centre piece of this establishment was a huge decaying combustion stove desperately lacking both the will to combust and the fuel necessary to provide such luxury. Optimism we were learning was the keynote to survival. O.K., so the accommodation was lousy — so what! Bread, also I suppose the German staff of life, was about to surface in the shape of one hundred grammes per man and — wait for it — this would be followed at 12 noon with an offering of sheer artistry and culinary cunning — a pea soup satisfyingly laced with, if you were lucky, a spoonful of barley. I got my bread but fell somewhat short on the barley.

It didn't take long for me to realise that I had joined a weird and strangely ritualistic society. Several choices were invitingly available to an extent that I suppose one could say that one was spoilt for choice. These inducements, not necessarily in order of precedence, were as follows:-

1. Join a party and, without any need to communicate, walk round and round the perimeter of the camp.

2. Join a food discussion group and torture those present with a graphic description of meals past or possibly fantasize over a futuristic meal.

3. Sit quietly and pick lice from the seams of one's clothing and lie about the total so that you could be one up against some other chap also hell bent on the complete and total annihilation of the lice Kingdom.

4. Join a German language class and be taught by someone enthusiastic enough to try, but woefully lacking in even a rudimentary knowledge of the language. (These self-designated 'teachers' were in abundance purely for the reason that in an effort to alleviate a general decline in morale, anyone deemed capable of providing the means to stimulate interest was rewarded with an extra slice of bread!).

5. Choice 5 could be rightfully described as the most profitable one and although I was acutely aware of a nagging feeling of hunger, I steadfastly refused to join the clammering hordes of would-be volunteers to be found waiting a respectable distance from the main gate every morning at 10 o'clock. The object of the exercise was to hopefully be selected by the guards to clean out the dog kennels which were situated outside but close to the gate. At this hour the dogs were taken from their quarters for a period of refresher training which allowed sufficient time in which to clean out the kennels in safety. The following part of these proceedings was the ultimate and sole reason for so willingly offering ones services. A German orderly, having checked the area for cleanliness, would return, passing along the line of kennels, conscientiously doling out a mouth-watering portion of mixed rice and meat in the bowl provided by each kennel. Immediately he disappeared so too did the dog's dinner. Some of the guards would good-humouredly laugh and look the other way whilst others, including one particular rabid specimen

would rush in, scream abuse and call an immediate halt to proceedings.

I say I wasn't *that* hungry, well, in the weeks to follow I did become hungry, in fact I became very hungry and on one occasion I was able to sample the delights of what can only be described as a 'dog's dinner'.

In this camp we were to experience many interesting events, some funny, some tragic, with others so strange as to border on the bizarre.

Take for example an escape tunnel being dug underneath the hut furthest distant from the main gate and needing a length of possibly sixty to seventy feet to clear the outside wire. This operation had the makings of a full-blooded effort, but engineered with little expertise and a woeful lack of secrecy. Volunteer workers and would-be escapees were openly recruited and a number in the pecking order for escape via the tunnel was given on recruitment. I believe my number was somewhere in the region of 180 and with no lack of tunnel diggers, I, along with many others, was given the job of collecting the earth removed from the digging and scattering it outside on the parade ground.

This scheme was to take up the whole of our time for many weeks until the tunnel was finally declared long enough to stretch way beyond the wire. On the night appointed for the breakout, a crowd, I should imagine well in excess of 300, had congregated in this single hut, normally overcrowded with its usual quota of between 60 and 80 men. Being unable to circulate after dark we had been instructed after the last roll call of the day to make our way in small groups to the confines of the hut which housed the tunnel. With a waiting time ahead of us optimistically figured out to be around six hours or so, the air quickly became polluted with the not too pleasant odours emanating from the seldom-washed bodies of such a large crowd. Imagine our despair when suddenly and without warning the door burst open and in came an excited posse of armed and very angry Germans who, without even going through the pretence of a search, went directly to the entrance of the tunnel.

Continuing to scream and threaten, the Kraut chased us out onto the now brilliantly lighted parade ground. Perplexed and uncontrollably angry as they were, nothing, it seemed, could prevent the soothing influence of a series of roll calls. We stood lined up in the ever-familiar ranks of 5 and they counted and counted and counted. To our way of thinking this was a completely useless exercise but for some unaccountable reason the German mind was totally obsessed with a need to count. Could this, we joked, be the only method whereby they could gain an unfair advantage over us? Another equally silly jibe passing along the lines suggested that they could be counting to decide whether or not it would be possible to put 300 men in bunkers designed to hold a maximum of six.

This, we decided, might well have been the case, but accepting the futility of the situation, they settled on the nearest six men who were summarily trotted off to the uninviting confines of the bunkers whilst we, the remainder, accompanied by a series of gutteral threats, yelps and oaths, were sent packing to our huts.

The following morning carried in its wake an inquest to decide what went wrong and the answer was not long in coming. Unbeknown to a lot of prisoners, one 'recently captured' prisoner proved to be half German. Under questioning he broke down and admitted his deception. He had, he admitted, told the Germans of the existence of the tunnel and they in turn had played a cat and mouse game waiting to be tipped off when the tunnelling had been completed. What later took place in that hut was something which wasn't talked about. I do know that there was a terrific commotion within that hut and that the Germans came in and effectively saved him from permanent injury. He was hiked off never to be seen again and we were left to wonder whether in fact he was a villain serving his own ends by receiving special treatment in exchange for his treachery or whether he was an English speaking German plant. He was the only one I ever came across although I'm told that this was not an altogether isolated instance. Still on the subject of escaping, I must mention the disastrous attempt made by a number of white South Africans who managed, or rather thought they had managed, to bribe a German guard who had promised to help them escape. Again the plan was crude and tainted with a desperation easy to understand. He had promised, on receipt of whatever payment was made, to let them know when he would next be on duty in the goon box and on that night he would leave a certain area of wire in darkness when sweeping the remainder of his area with the searchlight. The South Africans, blond and tall with a true Germanic appearance had gradually, or so they thought, gained his confidence by conversing with him in a mixture of Deutsch and Afrikaans. On the appointed night the first two prisoners, having almost reached the top of the wire, were hopelessly stranded when suddenly the lights were switched on, and they were instantly killed in a savage burst of automatic fire.

We, in the safety of our huts, could only listen and realise what had happened out there. The following morning during roll call we were to witness a terrible sight. The bodies of these two prisoners had been left caught up in the wire where they had died. It was only much later that their bodies were removed and taken, it is thought, for burial in the distant village cemetery.

The weather was showing an improvement although all the inmates were still feeling the cold. Food was at an all-time low and the lice were, if that was at all possible, being more troublesome than ever. Little wonder that desperate attempts were still being made to get out.

One objectionable and futile attempt was to climb aboard a horse-drawn cart which supported a huge metal container designed to hold the contents of the latrine trench – which was for health reasons emptied every day by an old Italian civilian – and hide within the confines of the tank. With the terrible amount of dysentery almost at times reaching epidemic proportions, one can readily imagine the situation of a would-be escapee standing in this filthy tank stoically submitting to the indignity of having this foul-smelling effluence poured over him. Such was the desperation to escape that drove men to suffer this vile and ineffective gamble. I knew many who tried this method only to be hauled out of the stinking morass when the lid of the container was removed for a final check prior to leaving the camp.

On an equally objectionable note, we had in our midst a number of so-called 'Racketeers'. These parasites could easily have claimed to have been more universally hated than the Germans – and here we are talking of our own people! They were a loathsome bunch possessing the unfortunate ability, like body lice, to inflict a maximum amount of irritation and misery on their less entrepreneurial associates. It will always remain a mystery as to exactly who they obtained their supplies from but manage it they did and, providing of course that one had the necessary means to purchase such goods, one could always obtain extra bread, a fresh egg or even a small leaf of tobacco.

Reluctantly, but nevertheless compulsively, we parted with our few personal possessions in exchange for the all too temporary satisfaction of that little extra item of luxury. Now it was also common knowledge that apart from their natural bent to exploit us, they were also terribly capable of exploiting each other and the old maxim of thieves falling out was not altogether new so far as these parasites were concerned. On one auspicious occasion, we were to gleefully witness a squabble between two of these despised con-men. The participants were, one would have thought, most unlikely confederates, on the one side we had a somewhat unwholesome looking guardsman − I can't remember his particular (or rather not so particular) regiment but I do recollect how unwholesome he looked − and his opponent, the mind boggles, was an American Ranger. One of these reptiles had accused the other of two-timing and a series of so-far harmless threats of violence were being bandied back and forth.

A huge crowd had rapidly formed and were now gleefully egging on these two reluctant heroes. We pushed them together time and time again but this failed to motivate either one. Anxious to appear the less cowardly, the guardsman eventually adopted a semi-crouching stance, half-heartedly inviting the Ranger to land the first blow. Worried, and thinking that if he were indeed to land the first blow, retaliation might swiftly follow, he therefore was exceedingly anxious to avoid the invitation to strike first. However, encouraged by we spectators he half-heartedly drew back his arm in readiness to land a weak blow in the direction of his adversary's head. The guardsman, sensing the likelihood of being hurt, immediately raised his arm and requested his opponent not to hit him on the left hand side of his mouth as he had a bad tooth there.

This last act was to cause an uncontrollable outburst of derision from the assembled spectators who, now surging forward and bodily lifting the two racketeers high above shoulder level ceremoniously carried them over to the latrine trench where they were both cheerfully consigned to those stygian depths.

Our stay here as I have previously said had its highs and its lows and one of the high features concerns the wealth of entertainment that was bought for a relatively cheap price – a slice of bread. We had a team of Maori performers who provided us with so much pleasure with their creative singing and dancing, we had Basuto troops from South Africa who sang unheard-of songs in unrecognisable English. We had an American, reputed to be a regular star radio performer, who would also sing for us and in particular a very professional rendering of 'Paper Doll', a song extremely popular during the war and a particularly poignant reminder of his own predicament.

The chap in the song had lost his girl and the chap singing the song had only received a 'Dear John' letter from his wife informing him of her defection to some well-heeled civilian just before he was taken prisoner. We had a series of remarkably well delivered lectures given by a former Englishman and later American serviceman who had roamed the States as a hobo for many years prior to the outbreak of war. So, as you can see, we had at times ample reason to count our blessings.

Bordering on the bizarre was our encounter with a top ranking German sports personality. It came to pass that on a certain early afternoon we were to find ourselves urgently summoned to the parade ground. Thinking that this could only be to attend for a snap roll-call, we were surprised to be ordered to form up in two long lines extending perhaps half way along the parade ground and facing each other with a space the width of an average road between the two lines. Not a hint of what was to follow increased our speculation although rumours, totally incredible in content, were rife: the Germans were ready to announce capitulation; the Pope was paying a surprise visit; Red Cross food parcels were to be distributed. We listened to all these rumours and speculated as to their accuracy, 'Why could it not be one of these?' we thought, optimistically noting that the guards, yes, even the Kommandant appeared to be in a particularly relaxed mood. However our hopes of an early release with a food parcel tucked underneath each arm and spiritually sustained with a personal blessing from the Pope himself somehow failed to materialise.

Startled back to reality by an unexpected blast of canned music issuing from a large raucous amplifier tucked beneath one of the goon boxes, we now fixed our gaze on a motorcade of vehicles which could be seen approaching the main gate,

now invitingly open to receive our visitors. The first car
was occupied by a group of cameramen, one of whom was
actively engaged in operating a movie-type camera mounted
on an enormous tripod and directed towards our assembled
columns. The second car, an impressive Mercedes-Benz was
occupied by a tall athletic type, well turned out in an expensive
suit and standing erect waving and smiling at us with an air of
friendly familiarity. Also travelling in the same car but seated
and obviously secondary in importance to this central figure,
was a group of aides at this moment in time apparently content
to sit undisturbed. Behind them came a third car also sporting
a camera crew.

In these hard times it did seem rather an odd thing to happen
to people like ourselves: to suddenly find ourselves centre stage
participants to a column of Mercedes-Benz which were now
beginning to move slowly between our ranks. The amplifier
had now reverted from music to speech and the disembodied
voice discoursing in perfect English went on to explain that
this personality, still smiling and waving, was none other than
Max Schmelling, the former holder of the World Heavyweight
title, who on June 22nd, 1938 was decisively beaten by the
reigning world champion, Joe Louis. Having delivered this
profound statement, the voice went on to plead for our
support in welcoming him. We were asked to wave and to
shake his hand. These pleas resulted in a marked lack of
enthusiasm, much to the disappointment of the cameramen
whose job it was to obtain good propaganda material for
distribution in some unspecified market. This reaction was
more likely than not anticipated, hence the presence of the
so far surplus bodies in the car carrying Schmelling. Their
function in life now became obvious as, delving under the
car seats, they emerged triumphantly holding aloft several
cartons of cigarettes which they proceeded to distribute to the
now more favourably impressed prisoners. This quite naturally
stimulated activity as the camp inmates, long starved of the
luxury of a cigarette, now grimly competed for the opportunity
to acquire one. They say everyone has a price but who but
ourselves would rate it as low as a cigarette. We didn't
come out of it very well but there again I don't suppose
Max Schmelling did either, as for a top sportsman, surely
he could have found some other way to further the German
war effort.

Shortly, following this encounter, an order came through to evacuate the entire camp and within a matter of days and clutching a piece of bread and a small ration of black pudding, we found ourselves again heading northwards towards yet another unknown destination.

CHAPTER THREE

Mantova (Dulag 339) – Brenner Pass – Munich – Moosburg

A Munich encounter

This, I know, is bound to sound very odd, but when we finally left Latrina behind us, we had positively no idea of the date, the day or even the time at which we moved on. Calendars were no longer a constant reminder of the passage of time and most timepieces, my own watch included, had been left in the care of unknown hands. In other words, they had been surrendered as the price of a piece of life-sustaining bread or for the fleeting pleasure of an item of sheer luxury, be it an egg or perhaps a wizened leaf of tobacco.

Rumour had it that the Allies had taken Rome and were now steadily pushing their way further north but the facts, as we knew them, lay in our present predicament. We didn't realise exactly what was ahead but we expected very little and in that respect we were bound to be right. We walked a lot and we rode a little, we cursed the heat of the day and the cold of the night but it was all a waste of time because nobody wanted to know.

I have mixcd feelings regarding my first and only visit to Florence. It was very early in the morning and we were being led along one of the main thoroughfares of this fair city fortunately sparsely patronised at this time by the local citizenry, no doubt on account of the early hour, but the truth was that we had been persistently calling for a break in order to relieve ourselves, but our guards, hell bent on maintaining their natural superiority with regards to ourselves, had so far paid absolutely no heed to our demands. However, possibly with a sardonic gesture, typical of the Hun's mentality, we were brought to a halt in the main street and invited to do whatever it was necessary to do. I can't remember who said that the only time you saw a German laugh was when he'd shot some bugger, but whoever he was, was guilty only of profoundly stating a bald fact.

By this time we were each carrying along a redundant stomach. This was disconcerting, particularly as we had, on so many occasions, jokingly remarked that our teeth had long since forgotten how to chew and now we were faced with having a stomach with nothing to digest.

Between Florence, Bologna and Mantova we passed through a countryside rich in fruit. We saw immense orchards bursting at the seams with a luscious profusion of peaches and cherries but our satisfaction, frustrating as it was, was to lie in the eye rather than the stomach. We completed our journey to Mantova by courtesy of an old Italian bus requisitioned recently and possibly permanently by the omnipotent Wehrmacht and thankfully seeing the back of the guards who, having counted and checked us into this camp which we rightly assumed to be a railhead transit camp, went thankfully upon their way. The camp was small and strangely lacking in prisoners but later we were to discover that this was accountably due to the frequent transportations from here into Germany. Our stay here was to be reasonably short and, apart from a single reservation, acceptably pleasant. This reservation, for want of a better word, applied most strongly to the presence of the German cookhouse Feldwebel who undoubtedly was the most loathsome creature in existence outside of Germany.

To explain this rabid feeling of revulsion towards this character it must be clearly repeated that we were hungry and, to a certain extent, wholly dependent upon this fat man's whims and fancies. Our only meal, apart from the infrequent provision of a small ration of bread, consisted of a mid-day issue of soup and this obese, highly volatile creature, was regrettably in a position to grossly overplay the role of being our daily tormentor.

His customary method of announcing the availability of our soup ration was by way of a large metal triangle situated outside the somewhat pretentiously-named cookhouse. Now, according to his mood and fluctuating on an irregular basis between playful contempt and sheer unbridled hatred, he would either order his terrified minions to produce the thin watery soup on which we relied so much or, as was quite often the case, he would issue an abrupt order, directed towards the inner regions of the kitchen, which would only too predictably end in producing from behind his back a water hose whose jet was powerful enough to bowl us over and give a most unwelcome soaking to boot. Therefore, as can be well imagined, our approach towards the kitchen was carried out with a certain degree of trepidation. In the months that followed we were to hear that, for him anyway, his exploits had been cut dramatically short by a stray burst of fire from an American fighter aircraft when the camp was straffed shortly, it seems, after we had departed.

Our ignominous departure from this transit camp was encouragingly highlighted by the unselfish concern shown by the local Italian women with an act of kindness one would think most probably re-enacted each time a transport left Mantova for Deutschland. These women, generous and courageous beyond belief, had lined themselves up along a narrow street leading to the railway sidings, each armed with either a bag of small bread rolls, known throughout Italy as 'Piccolo Panes', or with an apron held up at the waist holding a substantial supply of bread.

As our column approached they prepared to give us this bread as a parting gift before leaving on what they guessed would be a long tedious journey. Our guards, anxious to prevent any contact with us, began to push and strike out at these women who came upon us in waves. As one was brushed aside, another was there to take her place. Never before or since have I witnessed such concentrated determination. They came charging through our marching column handing out bread completely oblivous of the risk of bodily injury, and having crossed the column, with just enough time to take a deep breath, they were dashing through again this time from the other side.

The bread, a welcome addition to the sparse rations doled out prior to our departure from the camp, was doubly welcome but I think that the boost to our morale brought about by the simple act of caring by these women will never be forgotten. The only uninspiring feature of this encounter apart from the action of the Germans was the sad but not altogether unexpected sight of the many Italian males anxiously viewing proceedings from the safety of their upper floor windows.

Awaiting us at the sidings was the transport which was to take us through into Germany. This train, comprising a long line of large cattle-type wagons, was to be our home for, according to the rations handed out, the next three days. So far no engine had been coupled up, the wagon doors were wide open and each truck we could see contained a thin covering of straw spread evenly over the floor. There was a small barbed wire aperture high up on the side begrudgingly designed to give an absolute minimum amount of light and air and, although we couldn't see it at that time, we imagined, quite correctly, that there would be a similar opening on the other side. These wagons had quite plainly been used many times for the purpose of carrying prisoners both military and civilian, in fact it makes me shudder even now to think of the many times these particular trucks had been used to carry off so many innocents to those wretched concentration camps scattered around Germany and Poland. Each wagon had a special box-like arrangement perched high at the end and above roof level which would no doubt be manned by members of our escort already present and watching over us with an air of, 'I've done it all before'. To complete the picture, at the rear end of the train was an antiquated railway coach which, we imagined, would be used to accommodate the transport officer and off-duty guards.

We were unceremoniously loaded on board at the rate of forty men to a truck and, although it was to be many hours before we moved off, the doors were firmly closed and securely locked from the outside. Acclimatizing ourselves to this new situation demanded a great deal of co-operation and organisation from each of us. Toilet facilities, we were to discover, were to say the least totally inadequate. We had one standard size bucket between us and following a discussion, it was agreed that we adopt a strict rota system which would allow everyone in turn to stand by the window, sit on the floor and also to take a turn sitting beside the toilet bucket.

The heat penetrating the wagon from the outside plus the heat generated by so many bodies packed tightly together was already becoming overpoweringly oppressive and the small amount of water which we were carrying was in many cases being recklessly used far too quickly. This was in fact to become a very serious problem throughout our journey. It's all too easy to sit back in comfort and talk of self-discipline but it's an altogether different matter when one is actually faced with a need to implement this unnatural form of denial.

With regards to food, for example, we had many different theories and again it was a pure matter of choice. Did one immediately consume one's ration? Or did one perhaps live in anticipation of one glorious moment of satisfaction at the end of the day? Or perhaps, even more vexatious to the starved onlooker,was the so-called 'Sparrow Starver', in other words, a miser who would quite often be seen gloating and drooling at the mouth as he hesitantly picked his bread crumb by crumb making it last all day. I must confess that I belonged to the immediate consumer brigade because to my way of reasoning, providing one eats that which one has, it makes little sense denying oneself of that satisfaction. After all, supposing one is killed or injured? Supposing somebody should steal that food or what about the possibility of losing it? No, my firm immovable answer to this problem was always to eat because no matter which way one looked at it the bloody bread didn't grow any bigger. Impatiently waiting for this train to move off, coupled with the oppressive heat and the lack of air, was all beginning to have a strange knock-on effect on us. Bickering regarding one's right to more floor space or perhaps more air space was an obvious symptom of our general state. The toilet bucket was already starting to fill and one could scarcely fail to notice that already the straw around the bucket was beginning to get unpleasantly wet and untenable which in turn was likely to present a problem, as the response of the more fastidious prisoners was to crowd the other end of the wagon in order to get away as far as possible from the offending area.

Now to a certain extent, relating to the subject of guards, we, I would say, got lucky. We had, as I've recently remarked, spent an over considerable time locked up in this wagon and several people were already beginning to feel the effects of claustrophobia or heat exhaustion and were attempting to attract the attention of the guards hoping that the door could be opened to allow increased ventilation. To our eternal surprise, the door was eventually opened and one of our German guards, speaking in broken English, gave his name as Fritz and promised that he would try to provide us with a bucket of water.

True to his word, and shortly after disappearing for a little while, he was back grinning and sure enough carrying a bucket of water. He was the first Jerry we had so far encountered to express an active concern for our welfare and I'm afraid we rather took advantage of his good nature as not only did he make many trips to provide us with drinking water, but he also obligingly continued to play the role of a true Aquarian, a true water carrier beyond belief, and he never so much as murmured when we continued to abuse his good nature by asking for washing water. By this time several other guards had begun to follow his example even to the point of allowing two men per wagon to climb out and empty the slop bucket. In a short time we got to know Fritz very well. He sat on the edge of the wagon and told us that all the guards escorting this train had been at some time or other badly wounded, himself included, and we realised then that the bond of comradeship usually found to exist amongst front line troops did in fact extend even as far as the enemy. He spoke haltingly of his home in Westphalia, his attitude towards the war, his concern for his family, proudly exhibited as he fondly produced a selection of family photos for us all to see.

We had a real stroke of luck in this respect although a line of demarcation was very clearly drawn in so far as they were the gaolers and we were the gaoled and were graphically reminded that if we tried to make a run for it, then we would be shot. Shortly after this encounter, we felt the shuddering movement of an engine connecting with the wagons which provoked a hub of excited chatter from the prisoners, a scurry of frenetic activity from the guards now busily moving along the train checking the re-locking of the doors and, encumbered with their weapons, eventually climbing clumsily onto their roof top look-out positions.

The night was to prove both tiresome and exhausting as we jerked on, stopping and starting. We stood in sidings whilst troop and supply trains cautiously fed their way past, we rattled on for ages and at one stage we even went backwards. Guards could be heard either cursing their luck or exchanging odd snippets of conversation as they were relieved every so often. We had implemented the rota system on rest periods and towards dawn I found myself being shaken − I'd had a break sitting down and had somehow managed to drop off to sleep. There were a few cases of sickness either real or imagined and these chaps were given the right to a permanent piece of floor space. Stiff and bleary-eyed, I was still able to thread my way between the restless bodies lying either in the position which I had so recently vacated or standing around clutching at anything capable of providing a modicum of support. It was, I decided, quite eerie observing for the first time how, now that dawn was actually breaking, no sound could be heard other than the rattle of the train wheels as they contested every turn along the rails with a harsh grinding squeak and the faint muffled constant chug-chug of the engine as it laboured its way along its inclined path.

It was whispered − I don't know why − that we had just passed through a place called Trento and that we were now moving steadily northwards along a track sheltered on each side by what appeared to be tremendously high mountains which could only be the Italian Alps. From there we were to progress to the next sizeable station, Bolzano, where we were again generously supplied with water and had the added bonus of a mug of thin soup, very hot and very welcome and supplied by a number of ageing females of unknown nationality immaculately dressed in Red Cross uniforms. Here we waited allowing several trains to pass, including, we noted, a hospital train likely to reach the Fatherland much quicker than we would.

Fritz's popularity had reached a new height: not only was he the provider of yet another copious supply of water but, and this really impressed us, he gave half of his own bread ration and an apple to be shared as best as one could between those most in need. For the rest of the day we rumbled on in the customary spasmodic fashion. When you have literally no priority, the amount of waiting becomes interminable.

Towards late afternoon we were to experience an event that was to bring about a permanent rupture in our lately maturing relationship with Fritz.

It all started as we temporarily left the shelter of the mountains and made our way over an exposed area of undulating but, in comparison to the height of the mighty Alps, relatively flat ground. Suddenly and to our great anxiety, we realised that we were being straffed by a number of American fighter planes. Jerry being caught unawares had now recovered and, taking up the cudgel, was retaliating with several ineffective bursts from what sounded to be a light anti-aircraft gun accompanied by the familiar crackle of small arms fire.

We felt desperately exposed and were busily clammering at the door to be allowed out but no response was forthcoming.

The aircraft swooping down again for another crack at the train was a sight the Jerry didn't wish to see, and as one man they abandoned the train for the safety of a not too distant ditch leaving us to our fate. Fortunately for us, the Americans just couldn't get their act right and after another ineffective run, they nonchantly took off back to base.

Thanking our lucky stars for the Yanks' bad marksmanship was one thing but we felt incensed by the action of the enemy who had, in retrospect, behaved quite correctly in refusing to release us during this emergency. After all, given the opportunity, most of us would have scattered in all directions leaving Jerry holding the baby, or as in this case, an almost empty train. Anyhow, a council of war, hastily convened, declared that even though we would bear the brunt of the loss, there would be no more fraternizing with Fritz.

True to our word, that was exactly what we did. Childish though it may seem, we had of late been far removed from a state where we were able to exhibit a sense of independence and dignity and now that our dignity had supposedly been affronted, we were hell bent on making a moral if futile stand. Fritz, by the way, took it very badly but was unable to sway us away from our indignant stance. Even with a promise of lots more water, we decided that enough was enough.

The remainder of the journey which took us through the Brenner Pass into Austria gave us a brief view of the Inn Valley then onto Innsbruck when a brief halt in the station allowed us a glimpse of this most picturesque town spreading its wings, or so it seemed, along the entire length of the main street, the Maria Theresa Strasse. The war, I'm sure, had somehow contrived purely out of respect for its apparent air of sanity to bypass this idyllic scene. Granted, all over the station, glaringly displayed, were reminders that this, the railway, was still a very functional part of the war. Posters reminded the unwary, 'Feind hört mit', or similar words to that effect which prompted an unrecognised voice in the truck, flaunting, no doubt, his superior education to advise us in a knowledgeable way that those words broadly speaking meant that 'The Enemy is Listening' − a reminder to keep a still tongue. Other posters reminded the masses that for some unknown reason, 'The wheels must roll for Victory', etc. etc. The main advert to hold my gaze was the one appealing for the 'Winter Help Fund' which to my way of thinking amplified a chink in the enemies' armour. It was an appeal for used items of clothing much needed by the troops on the Russian Front to offset the bitter cold of the long and harsh Russian winter to come. Surely, I thought, this Nazi regime, boastfully claiming its men and equipment to be the finest in the world, could scarcely be begging for cast-off clothing?

Our next stop at Munich station caused a ripple of excitement. I've only seen this station on the one occasion but it stands out most vividly as a huge bustling affair, drab and bleak like most large railway stations are, but taking advantage of its ample wall and roof space, the place was absolutely festooned with the brilliant red, white and black swastika flags crudely flaunted from every conceivable perch. One full blast of Wagnerian music was followed by another one, steel helmet and breast-plated police were everywhere checking soldiers and civilians alike, and all this going on whilst I was lucky enough to be taking a breather by the open ventilator.

Now the most peculiar thing about this large station is the fact that, so far as I can remember, the platform at which our train was standing was not only terribly long but also crescent shaped. Granted our vision was to a certain degree restricted, but I do know that positioned as we were, roughly speaking, in the middle of the train, we could see neither the front nor the rear portion of the train due to this long sweeping curve. Now, standing immediately in front of us on the platform was a civilian, shabbily dressed in ill-fitting clothing. It's difficult after all this time to even attempt to give a better description than that which I have just given – in fact, in one word, I'd describe him as 'nondescript' and that was just how he appeared to us.

A sudden spur-of-the-moment decision to sound him out for a cigarette was equally inexplicable but we felt that, gasping for a smoke, we'd got nothing to lose. Our request, however, not having exactly fallen on deaf ears was greeted by the loudest and most prolonged torrent of abuse we had so far encountered. He just didn't say 'No', he spelt it out, he spat at us and we, in a moment of carefree abandon, gleefully led him on provoking him to the likely extent of terminal apoplexy. We shouted and he, not to be outdone, shouted louder. He screamed and raged shaking his fists until, thoroughly exhausted, he mentally collapsed like a pricked balloon.

The crowd that had gathered was now beginning to move away. Even a red-faced military policeman who had sauntered over in time to catch the tailend of this incident had, with a final shrug of his shoulders, walked away, and we too, now that the train began to pull out, were also on the move. Stung into action by the slow ponderous movement of the train, the man was again raging and gesticulating. Somehow he managed to keep abreast of our wagon until we had almost reached the end of the platform and when we were completely out of view from the centre section of this long half-moon shaped platform, his attitude suddenly changed and, delving into his pockets, he pulled out several packets of German cigarettes, stuck them one by one through the barbed wire, called out in good English, 'Good Luck, lads' and immediately disappeared.

It's a long time ago since that happened and although there must be an answer to it, I'm afraid that I can't even speculate as to the truth. Was he a crank? An escaped prisoner? Or perhaps a genuine Anti-Nazi? It's no good guessing, I'll never know.

There were so many things we didn't know. For instance, we didn't know that on leaving Munich our present journey was almost at an end. We didn't know then that we were bound for a prison camp some twenty-five miles up the road from Munich near to the village of Moosburg and neither did we know at that time that Dachau, the infamous concentration camp, was not very far away from us.

CHAPTER FOUR
Moosburg – Bavaria (Stalag VIIa)
... *Russians, Religion, Rackets*

There was no welcoming committee. We alighted at a rickety, wooden siding and at first glance decided we didn't like it. So far as the eye could see, there was nothing but a flat uninteresting landscape. Granted, there was the odd farm or two scattered around but the huge camp visible at the far end of the road on which we were now walking suddenly seemed less than inviting.

As we approached the main entrance we were visibly shaken by the air of cold efficiency of this place. Here we had our first proper Stalag, nothing at all like the late Dulag 32 at Latrina. We were on a metalled road still quite a distance from the camp entrance but already we were passing long lines of German barracks. There appeared to be guards everywhere being drilled or chased around on physical training and more easily distinguished was a private army of administration personnel busily engaged in dashing about and more likely than not doing nothing.

Impressively depressing was the ornate wooden structure functioning as a cross beam above the huge fortified gates to the camp. It was a huge, solid block of wood skillfully carved in heavy Bavarian style and depicting a bedraggled column of defeated British and French soldiers dispiritedly shuffling along into captivity and above all this was a caption which read, 'Nach Berlin'. I suppose seeing this convinced us, that is if we were still in need of being convinced, that the Hun had a most perverse brand of humour. Another thought flashing through my mind was to the effect that if this camp had indeed been employed as a Stalag since perhaps the First World War, would this reflect an improvement on past performance or perhaps an even further deterioration in basic standards. Either way it was an offer we couldn't refuse.

We were lousy, unwashed and not exactly palatable to look at. I think we arrived here about mid June and we hadn't managed a hot wash since the previous March. Jerry, however, was aware of this and we were packed off to a separate compound to be isolated until given a clean bill of health. This was a relatively small prison within a very large prison and Jerry, paranoid beyond the call of duty, insisted on our removing all our clothing before submitting, if that is the word for it, to a two minute long hot shower timed and supervised by a fat Fritz with a whistle in one hand already half poised to his lips which, I remember thinking, shook or trembled loosely like a bloodhound's jaws. In the other hand he held a stop watch. One whistle meant a scalding stream of hot water would cascade down upon our unprepared bodies and be turned off at the piercing command of another blast from his whistle, long before we had been able to muster a token lather from the most peculiar soap I'd ever encountered.

This exercise alone was sufficient enough to chasten an ox but an even greater refinement was to follow — we were checked in every crook and cranny for lice. It was stupid, come to think of it, 'Why, after all, look for something we'd all got plenty of?', we thought. With whoops of fiendish delight a malicious, sadistic posse of medical orderlies swooped upon us armed with razor blades and a rather objectionable type of de-lousing powder — I remember, these generous-sized packets of a peculiarly revolting whitish-grey powder were clearly labelled, 'kleider laus pulver'. During our stay in Deutschland we were to experience many shortages but a shortage of this commodity was seldom to be observed.

Anyhow, the razor blades helped dig out the more tenaciously entrenched creatures who had founded an ever-increasing family of self-help communities beneath our skin and by self-help, I mean they helped themselves to us. They were reluctant to leave the warmth and sustenance made freely available by our inadequately defended bodies, the razor blades seemed to fetch out more blood than lice and the powder, supposedly designed to decimate these ravenous hordes, seemed merely to provide them with a second course — they loved it.

Pausing to gain breath after suffering this latest onslaught on our dignity, we were suitably feted with a hand-out of the niggardly 100 gramme ration of bread and, for a change, a remarkably thick, pleasant tasting potato soup.

A senior British N.C.O., an inmate of long standing would be my guess, was brought into the compound to explain to us our position. We were, he said, in the quarantine enclosure of this camp which was officially known as Stalag VIIa and situated close to the small town of Moosburg. Pending a final clearance of infection and following an issue of new uniforms provided by the British Government and delivered by courtesy of the Swiss Red Cross, we would be formally, and in accordance with the Geneva Convention, registered as Prisoners of War.

That is exactly what happened. We got our new uniforms but, although it was absolutely marvellous to feel clean clothing next to the skin, we felt very self conscious by the way the Jerry insisted on marking them. On the back of each tunic was stencilled a huge caption which read 'K.G.F.', the equivalent in German to 'P.O.W.' and meaning, in full, Kriegsgefangener. That was enough for starters but simply not enough to satisfy the authorities who had decreed that a large diamond also stencilled in brilliant red should be clearly marked on the right hand thigh of the trousers.

Our next trip was for 'mug shots', which, although a comparatively simple operation, almost resulted in a comedy of deliberate errors. First we had the civilian photographer, lovingly caressing an ancient and much-used camera on a huge tripod and aided by his assistant, zealously engaged in ensuring that we should in turn stand on the large X which had been chalked on the ground. In addition to this task of monumental importance he also had charge of a piece of board measuring about 18″ long by approximately 4″ wide on which a permanent half series of numbers was already transcribed. In this instance the first three numbers read 130 with the remaining numbers being erased and amended with a stick of chalk as each of us in turn stepped forward to be photographed holding up the board in a position just below the chin. My own number turned out to be 130485. Much to the annoyance of the guards, supposedly present to supervise the smooth running of the operation, many photographs taken that day would most surely have qualified for a place even in a German chamber of horrors. With protruding tongues, closed eyes and various other grotesque facial contortions, we gleefully struggled to reduce the assembled officials to desperately contemplate suicide. The next phase in the system was finger printing. This was carried out to the almost visible relief of the Kraut without any further disturbance, however our response to their question as to what our civilian occupation was, almost caused them to sit on their hind legs and howl. We registered as waiters – 'waiting for the war to end' – but they, abysmally devoid of humour, could only scathingly remark that they thought that only the French and Italians were waiters. A prize-giving ceremony was to terminate any further hapless proceedings when each of us was given a small metal identity disc with our registered number already stamped on it. As a footnote and much to our annoyance we were called back only a few days later to have our mug shots taken for a second time and this time with no protruding tongues etc. Still being left to stew in this small isolation compound was beginning to have a claustrophobic effect on us. The lice population had been decimated thanks to the onslaught of the frequently over-zealous attentions of the enthusiastic but woefully inadequately trained medical orderlies, but we were now beset by an outbreak of dysentery which caused some concern to the Krauts who, with their obsession as usual laced with paranoiac overtones, absolutely and flatly refused to allow us entry to the main camp.

That they should be so lucky, we thought whilst we, queuing frantically for a space in the toilet line, would curse the inadequacy of the system. Here we had possibly 150, men most of whom were suffering severe stomach cramps yet unable to obtain relief. The latrine trench measured possibly 20 feet or so in length with a single pole supported at each end by a make shift trestle which provided the sole means of support. It could only be attributed to the wonders of modern science that this pole, bearing an ever constant weight of possibly a dozen precariously perched sagging bodies, never actually broke consigning its groaning regulars to the murky depths although, and always with a friendly cheer, we would witness a chap unable to maintain his balance pass unceremoniously into the dubious delights of this evil-smelling pit.

With the resilience of youth, recovery was not long coming and with the benign blessings of the powers-that-be we were begrudgingly despatched to the confines of the main camp. To our astonishment, we had so far failed to realise the enormous size of this Stalag, and we were positively amazed at its actual expanse. Each nationality represented within the camp seemed to have its own compound. Adjoining ours was the Russian compound whose inmates were in an appalling condition. These ragged gaunt creatures starkly resembled the living dead. Most seemed unable to do little more than sit or lie around their huts, whilst a few, slightly stronger than the other unfortunates, tended to congregate by the wire separating our two camps, mutely holding out their hands hoping for however little we had to spare.

Apparently death in there was nothing more than a common occurrence. Living with it had obviously become the norm but to us it was a distressful sight to witness the daily routine of bodies being taken out for burning or burial on a simple overloaded hand cart.

Adjoining the bottom of our compound was a unit which held a number of officers including at that time the Lord Lascelles, who, I believe, was to end up in Colditz as a Prominente. On the far side, separated by the main road, were compounds housing Americans, Dutch, Belgian, Italian and French Nationals. Most prisoners were securely accommodated within their own territory although the French and Italians, most of whom had given their parole, were allowed relatively free movement both inside and outside their camp.

Our huts were sparsely furnished as could only be expected although we had a little more space between the beds than that which we had in Latrina. The general conditions seemed fractionally more comfortable although that feeling was possibly due to the fact that the weather was now quite hot and the previously uncomfortable and unhygenic habit of sleeping fully clothed could, for the present time, be dispensed with. Roll calls were still the main and most disagreeable feature of the day. Long and boring, equally frustrating both to the Germans and ourselves, they just couldn't get it right. Throughout my stay in this Godforsaken country, it continued to amaze me how people, considered to be so righteously positive and efficient as they, could seldom manage a simple head count. The more they failed, the more angry they got and the longer we stood around, the more angry we got until their shouted threats competing with our shouted insults would result in a stalemate and pretending to have finally got it right, we would be dismissed.

One day, after a particularly long and frustrating roll call, we returned to our huts where, to our amazement, we were to find a brand spanking new copy of Hitler's 'Mein Kampf', plus a pamphlet inviting us to join up with the Germans in their struggle to defeat the Russians. We were told that the 'British Free Corps', as it was known, was a military unit recruited solely from British P.O.W.s. No volunteer would be called upon to fight against his own countrymen but solely against the evil spread of Communism. It went on to say how we would be trained in the use of German weaponry and how our German uniform would carry a Union Jack flash on each shoulder to prove our nationality. Anyone interested was asked to make themselves known to any guard member who, having passed on his request, would treat the matter as confidential and no information concerning that individual would be passed on to his friends.

Needless to say there were no known volunteers, in fact I believe the advertising campaign was so ineffectual as to succeed only in attracting a few rebellious malcontents who, had they not been taken prisoner, would most likely have fallen foul of our own authorities. According to press reports, circulated after the war finished, it does seem pretty certain that the only battles the British Free Corps ever participated in were those fought between themselves in the more sleazy wartime bars of Berlin.

I suppose that in a way we were lucky being in this camp as, relatively speaking, it was situated within a reasonable distance of Switzerland, and therefore the transportation of Red Cross food parcels was in no way as restricted as it was in camps placed much further afield in places like Silesia and Poland. The German railway system had for a long time been taking a tremendous pounding from the Allied Air Forces and as can be readily appreciated, prisoners in distant camps were, in the main, committed to a much greater shortage of these life-giving parcels than those fortunate enough to be situated in camps such as Stalag VIIa.

It's hard to credit, but even the supply of these welcome gifts was destined to create a problem. The very first one I received came by courtesy of the Canadian Government. They were absolutely invaluable and contained so many nutritious items of food such as raisins, tea, meat loaf, powdered egg and a tin of powdered milk with, I remember, the brand name Klim (milk spelt backwards) prominently displayed on the side of the can. In addition to all those goodies was a small sealed tin of butter and as a method of extracting maximum benefit from this food, bearing in mind the lack of cooking facilities, we indulged quite unashamedly in what was universally called a 'Klim Bash'. Now to make a 'Klim Bash' didn't necessarily require a great deal of expertise or inventiveness, it simply meant concocting what might seem to be a revolting mixture of powdered milk, raisins, butter and meat to which sufficient water was added to produce, after the whole concoction was thoroughly stirred, a satisfying if somewhat repulsive looking meal. I did start off by saying that the availability of these parcels was sufficient enough to create a problem. This problem was, after all, self-inflicted, the reason being mainly due to our close proximity to the French and Italian compounds. The inmates of these compounds were able, within limitations, to obtain fresh food such as perhaps eggs, bread and potatoes from the farms where they worked and they, lacking the type of food recently made available to ourselves, allowed for the creation of an international black market.

Unfortunately, however, we could only make contact during a brief visit on a Sunday morning to their compound which, by chance, also housed the hut which served as an inter-denominational church when, motivated by a tacit agreement on exchange values, we would surreptitiously carry out our illicit transactions before being escorted back to our own compound.

Outings to Church, it must be understood, reached an all time high in the popularity charts. Not only did we seek to attend the C. of E. service but also R.C., Methodist, Baptist and, I believe, had we not left when we did, then I could well imagine some furtive entrepreneur pressing for a service for Buddhists and Seventh Day Adventists. So after all, apart from the many undignified scrambles violent enough on occasions to deter all but the strongest heart, it was both gratifying and stimulating to the previously despairing army of resident padres now totally convinced by this upsurge of religious awakening that our fervent desire to participate could result in nothing less than a spiritual revival seldom before witnessed.

Selfish and self-centred as we were, with a recent history all too vivid of shortages and deprivation we still remembered to pass over the wire to the starving Russians however much we could spare. We were, I suppose, beginning albeit slowly to learn the art of living together as a unit rather than as individuals. Shortages, I'm sorry to say, had so far tended to alienate us against each other but now, after a series of setbacks and associated problems we were noticeably moving towards becoming a more caring, protective society. Maybe a long stay in one prison camp would become unacceptably soul destroying with its lack of change and interest and, I suppose, more than anything else its all-pervading air of depression. However, far be it from me to dwell on that subject as, without warning, we were ordered to once more be ready to retrace our steps in the general direction of the rail siding.

CHAPTER FIVE

Mühlberg – Saxony (Stalag IVb)

As one door closes ...

Fortified by the distribution of a day's ration of bread and blutwurst meant that no matter where we might finish up it should certainly take no longer than two days to get there and of course we also had what was left of our last Red Cross parcel which, unfortunately, due to the unpredictable whims of the vigilant Krauts, had suffered at their hands by their spiteful action of piercing all unopened tins with a bayonet. This in itself was a cruel blow since we had managed to save a little surplus for the proverbial rainy day, and this now meant that the entire contents, particularly in view of the current hot spell of weather, must more or less be consumed immediately – one up to Jerry!

It was an uneventful journey. We had the usual baying commands to either get on the bloody train or get off it and on our frequent demands for water the usual bleat, 'Es gibts kein'. We knew they had got nothing but we were only just beginning to realise that when they continually repeated that they had nothing, they were quite often referring to the vacant area in the head and between the ears. These guards were different, they were niggling, under or oversized, elderly, but for all that we were firmly convinced that it would fetch a real laugh if only they were given the opportunity to shoot one of us. We passed through Nuremberg, the scene of many of Hitler's triumphs, and although unknown to us at that time, soon to be the scene of his henchmen's demise. We passed through Chemnitz although I don't know why I'm telling you all this, it just looked an awfully grubby place to hurry past. Finally, and to our immediate relief, we settled at a small siding which almost ashamedly admitted through the medium of a tatty sign hanging precariously askew to be Mühlberg. This area, flat and inhospitable, was situated, I believe, roughly half-way between Leipzig and Dresden with seemingly its only claim to notoriety being that it was the site of our latest Stalag, Stalag IVb. It also boasted an airfield from which a shrill whining noise so far alien to our ears was heard many times during our brief stay. It was a jet engine that made this strange unnatural noise and was, or so we were later to be told, the prototype model of the first German jet plane being rigorously tested by one of their leading test pilots, Hanna Reitsch.

Our induction to this Stalag was indeed unusual and a mind-boggling experience to boot. We were once more taken into an isolation area separate from the remainder of the camp and, without further ado, found ourselves being unceremoniously ushered into a rather large building thoughtfully broken down into a series of compartments. The first compartment, stripped of all furnishings, was our first port of call. We were ordered to undress and place our clothing in a corner which served as a collection area before proceeding to the next section which housed a shower unit where, after the second quickest cleansing on record, we were directed through the only door left open into the next section.

This section, we were surprised to see, was manned by a number of unwholesome looking Italian P.O.W.s uneasily standing alongside a line of tables which sported a few basic items of medical equipment such as bottles of iodine, a number of syringes, an open box of enormous and wicked-looking needles and several boxes holding small bottles of some kind of serum. It was pretty obvious that this was not going to be our day. There was no possible chance to duck out of line as the door through which we had just entered had been securely locked and, still standing naked, we could see our clothing, discarded, fumigated and awaiting our collection once we had run the gauntlet of these unlikely-looking medical orderlies. As the line of P.O.W.s moved forward, a series of indignant yelps and curses could be heard from those ahead in the column who were now being subjected to this latest assault on their person.

I had already slid back to the rear of the column, possibly thinking, quite wistfully, I suppose, that perhaps the serum would run out before my turn came or in the vain hope that perhaps, with all the commotion going on ahead, it might just be possible to walk through unnoticed, but that wasn't to be. The first Itie, clutching a bottle of iodine in the one hand and a ball of cotton wool in the other, moved slowly along the queue dabbing a liberal dosage of iodine high on the chest and, as we approached the tables, other staff standing with loaded needles already poised in line with our recently iodine-annointed chest, drove in painfully and solidly before releasing the anti-typhus serum. These needles, huge and blunt, were not even wiped clean, let alone sterilized before being plunged into the next victim which seemed odd, particularly so when one considers how extremely paranoid Jerry was on matters of infection.

I think, on the whole, that the philosophy of the Kraut was that nothing should be attempted unless it was first made difficult. Take our clothing as yet another glaring example: we'd only been given a brand spanking new uniform a matter of a few weeks earlier after being cleansed of lice, and yet now we were back to a further bout of cleansing plus innoculation and the fumigation of our new clothing. We never got our original uniform back. Here was just a mountain of clothing from which we had to try and select whatever seemed most likely to fit.

Emerging into the sunlight of a glorious sunny day absolved of everything save, perhaps, our mortal sins, life began to take on a new meaning, the rich tapestry of life syndrome all over again, I thought. First impressions, not always, we had so frequently discovered, a necessarily accurate assessment were, in this case, a good omen. This was a good camp, the atmosphere was good and a throng of old lags waiting to greet us with calls of 'Anyone from London?', 'Anybody from Liverpool?' and so forth were met with an appropriate response. I was immediately taken under the wing of two local chaps, Bill Coates, an R.A.F. Air gunner shot down sometime past and 'Ginger' Mullins, a prisoner since Dunkirk.

Both these chaps proved themselves to be exceptionally good friends and 'Ginger', actively engaged with the camp concert party, promised to arrange – and did – a special concert for we people who had just arrived. They gave me socks for which I'm eternally grateful as a spare pair of socks was always a most welcome luxury.

The standard of food here, although not particularly good, could almost be described as adequate. There had been an issue of Red Cross parcels but unfortunately for us, it seems we'd again missed out. 'Ginger', however, was one of nature's survivors with an instinctive aptitude for being one move ahead and due to his good offices, I was to be the frequent and grateful recipient of many an extra piece of bread deviously liberated by him from the inner confines of the camp kitchen.

The football pitch was, if I remember correctly, one of the outstanding features of this camp. Well tended but, at least during our stay, never utilised. The food may have been just about adequate but apparently insufficient to stimulate a desire to work off surplus energy. Rumour had it, whether or not true, I do not know, that prior to its becoming a mainly French and British P.O.W. camp, it had previously been used to house Russian Prisoners who, unfortunately due to the callous attitude of the Germans, had been wiped out to a man by a tragic outbreak of typhus. Hence this rather pretentious football pitch which we were told on good authority, covered the mass grave of several thousand Russians.

During the day with very little to do other than sit around, many of us were to make a practice of visiting the inmates of several of the other huts. This venture on our part served a dual purpose as, ignoring the painfully obvious intent to scrounge and take advantage of whatever opportunity came along, we were quite subconsciously feeling a need to become an accepted part of this community. Over the past few months I think it could safely be said that we had, purely by force of circumstance, become not only selfish but on frequent occasions openly hostile towards each other and terribly inward looking.

This camp, with a friendly generous outlook was, I'm sure, instrumental in effecting a drastically-needed change of attitude. The concert party, for example, proved a remarkable success, particularly so when one considers the painstaking preparation and the highly dedicated degree of inventiveness which was required to make such a production possible. The costumes and scenery, handmade and painted or dyed, were of an astonishingly high quality and were matched only by the expertise and enthusiasm of the entire cast. One particularly outstanding performer that day was a young R.A.F. chap, a surviving member of an aircrew shot down, if my memory serves me correctly, near Frankfurt. He sang for us in a voice several times better than many of the overpaid and under qualified professionals of today. One song entitled, 'All the things you are', was received with a tremendous surge of applause, in fact it went down so well that he wasn't allowed to leave the stage without an encore. Sadly, many, in fact too many years have gone by, but still on the rare occasion when I hear that song played, I slip away quietly down memory lane way back to that afternoon of unbelievable peace and comradeship.

We were invited to circulate freely amongst the huts occupied by the long serving prisoners captured at Dunkirk who appeared, in most cases, to be resigned to sitting out the remainder of the war in semi-isolation. Many I spoke with seemed blissfully content and surrounded by an air of acceptance that to a certain extent was already beginning to rub off on ourselves. So far in my life, being young simply meant that one allowed little or no time to think. Thinking, I had decided long before, was an activity solely designed to keep old men happy. Yet here, in this strange, almost limbo-like situation, I was to find myself being taught to think by these people.

School, in those so-called formative years, had failed to impress. The standard of teaching, woefully inadequate, was matched only by our lack of enthusiasm and attentiveness and when, at the age of 14, I ran out of that grim prison-like citadel of learning for the very last time, I experienced an overpowering sense of joy seldom since recaptured. Abysmally ignorant, it had taken many years and a prison camp to produce in me an awareness to think creatively. Regrettably we didn't stay over long in Mühlberg but educationally the most rewarding feature of that brief yet pleasant stay was the emergence of this almost overwhelming need to mentally expand. As a group we had discussed and indeed argued many subjects, in particular the relative differences between talking and conversing. Talking, we agreed, was simply a method of expressing a usually one-sided opinion whereas conversing, we had learned, was a means of exchanging and evaluating an opinion. I suppose it made some impression on me because from that day onwards, I was to make a great effort to avoid being classified as a 'talker'.

Another unforgettable character whose name regrettably escapes me, was responsible for promoting many hours of good-humoured entertainment by way of his graphic observations of the comings and goings centred around a small close-knit community situated somewhere in the darkest depths of rural Wiltshire, where, until the outbreak of World War II, he had spent his early life.

There was, it seemed, an altogether too gay Lothario residing in their midst and the villagers, with of course the obvious exclusion of the young females on whom he so generously bestowed his affections, felt prompted, no doubt more by jealousy rather than downright indignation, to cast a baleful eye on his increasingly frequent nocturnal adventures. It came to pass, however, that the bounds of decency were to be irrevocably breached when it became painfully clear that the local barmaid was becoming visibly heavy with his child.

A council of war chaired by the village elders elected on a plan to inflict maximum retribution against this unholy despoiler of the female species. Anxious to learn more of the method of punishment meted out against this wicked transgressor, we were absolutely astounded when amidst a scene of complete disorder caused by the re-telling of the climax of this story, our friendly storyteller was heard to say, 'We fixed the bugger, we pinned a condom on his front door with a note that read, "Use one of these next time"'!

Rumour had it that we were about to be shipped out. Every stage so far was nothing more than a step nearer to a Kommando or labour camp and that I did not want. I was relaxed here and had little desire to move. However, little choice was available. For a start, someone suggested a faked illness as this sometimes resulted in success and anyhow, with little or nothing to lose, why not give it a go? That is exactly what I did. I reported sick and I was summarily ordered to present myself for examination by the German doctor, Stabsartz Schmidt, on his next visit to the camp.

Invited into his surgery on the appointed day, I felt quietly confident that I was about to register a success. He was a very elderly, painfully correct man, genuinely concerned, I thought, to hear of my bouts of giddiness and total deafness. My graphic account of the numbing ear pains I so stoically suffered almost, I felt, reduced him to tears. My Oscar-winning performance I now knew had paid off. He indicated with a movement of his hands that the examination I had undergone was over and that I was free to leave. Scarcely able to conceal my delight, and knowing how well I had performed, I was confidently moving towards the door when I was surprised to hear him say very softly and in perfect English, 'Please leave the door open' — I did, and the very next day I was on the move, again one step nearer to the work camps.

This time, fortified as always with a day's ration of bread and black pudding, we took two days to arrive at our next destination. Our journey, packed in like sardines, was as uncomfortable as the previous ones. There was little chance to sit, let alone sleep, and the hours had an awful knack of dragging by. The conditions being endured by the Jerry were indeed little better than our own. Someone called out from his viewing position by the exposed ventilator that we had just passed through a large station called Breslau, gleefully adding that a fairly large area of that town appeared to have taken a severe hammering from the air.

The railway, in general, hadn't really fared any better than the local townships, hence the need for our journey covering a matter of 150 miles or so dragging on into a two day marathon. A final halt was however to settle it all and we were gratefully obliged when, accompanied by a series of loud bangs on the side of the wagon, the doors were flung open and we were ordered out. It was, we were about to discover, Lamsdorf Stalag 344.

Set in the flat wastelands of Silesia, Lamsdorf looked just as grim and uninviting as it turned out to be. A huge camp divided, it seems, into three main sections, there was the main camp housing many Nationals but excluding Russian prisoners. The second section, set some distance from the main camp and noticeably isolated from all else, contained the Russians who were having a very bad time of it. Neither Russia nor Germany gave any quarter to prisoners of war. The plight of these starving hordes was indeed desperate to the extent that the third section of this huge prison camp contained nothing more than a cemetery which was used purely and simply to bury the Russian dead. Our treatment here at times bordered almost on the callous yet it could scarcely be compared in any way to the diabolically inhumane treatment meted out to these unfortunates. No attempt was made to cover up the atrocities perpetrated here. Prisoners capable of work would be worked to death whilst those unable to work would be starved to death, whilst in between, a succession of unpremeditated shootings and beatings would accelerate the now normal chain of events more efficiently. The disturbing picture of these filthy, wasted and dejected beings will remain for the rest of my days. Food, as such, was non-existent and it was rumoured, I believe, on good authority, that cannibalism within their compound was rife. As a point of callous intimidation the Germans frequently adopted the practice of releasing their vicious guard dogs into the Russian compound simply to terrorise the prisoners but, after several of these brutes failed to return, the practice was discontinued — they'd been eaten!

Our own entry into this camp was greeted with an unnecessary degree of intimidation as, sapped of energy after the somewhat gruelling trip from Mühlberg, we fell foul of a detachment of Krauts who not only insisted on a strip search but also kept us that way for a long time. Searching amongst our belongings, they confiscated any small item which in their tiny minds might be of use in an attempt to escape. Small pieces of metal ground to provide a cutting instrument, crude but suitable for hacking at a piece of bread, were confiscated. Several chaps were even denied the use of a number of short lengths of rope or string which, until then, had merely held together a few pathetic possessions. Anyone lucky enough to have secreted a tin of food now found their luck had run out. It was either seized as being a possible aid to escape or, at the least, pierced to ensure immediate consumption.

We didn't like what we saw here. It was so huge as to be mind-boggling. Several thousand prisoners were milling around with little to do other than stare at us as we finally made a decidedly undramatic entrance to this dump. It was on our second day there that I was to meet up with Lofty, a tall gentle chap with a rich sense of humour and concern that was to stand me in good stead during the weeks that followed. Lofty Banks had served with the Royal Engineers, and prior to joining up had been, I should imagine, quite content to go his way as a builder in Stone, Staffordshire.

Surprisingly enough this was our first meeting although he was registered as a P.O.W. at the same time that I was registered, in fact he was slightly ahead of me in the queue at Moosburg. I know this for a fact as my prison number was 130485 and his was 130008. Camp food, we had already discovered, was to say the least a bit thin on the ground, but fortunately a small consignment of food parcels had been delivered and we were to have an issue of one parcel between four men.

Lofty, looking around for three others to share with, approached me and we in turn approached two others and that, as I say, was my first meeting with Lofty.

Shortly afterwards we were sitting on the ground picking lice, if I remember correctly, out of our clothing. The warm days, a lack of adequate dietary needs plus a general weakness had again brought back these pests to feast on our bodies. We had subconsciously if somewhat begrudgingly accepted the presence of these little whatsits, apart from inflicting upon them the odd punitive measure which anyhow did little or nothing to prevent their remarkable rate of procreation. I mention this simply to illustrate the basic beginning of my friendship with Lofty. Basic it was, otherwise how better could one possibly cement a friendship than through the joint and ultra personal occupation such as that in which we were so diligently involved.

I can't remember who the other two members of our temporary syndicate were and anyhow they were there purely for the purpose of forming a group of four brought together for no reason other than to share a food parcel. The huts, constructed of timber and capable of housing an uncomfortably large number of prisoners, were particularly unpleasant places in which to spend one's days. Somehow the heat from the sun appeared to generate into an even higher temperature inside the dingy confines of these barrack huts and that, coupled with the stench of not-too-often washed bodies encouraged Lofty and me to spend as much time as possible out of doors.

It was during times such as these that I was able to learn of the interesting and unusual events that had led to Lofty being in this particular camp. Whilst serving with the Royal Engineers, he had unfortunately been left behind in Greece when the Allied Armies, unable to compete against the massive onslaught of the German Army, were forced to evacuate. Lofty had made his way towards the coast hoping to be picked up by friendly Greeks, thinking perhaps that they would somehow manage to get people like him over to Cyprus.

However, as things turned out, the friendly Greeks weren't really friendly and he had met up with a considerable amount of abuse, very little food and an even less chance of assistance.

Several weeks later, almost exhausted, he came upon a village which turned out to be more hostile than usual and within a very short period of time someone had reported his presence to the Jerries and an indignant Lofty was very quickly rounded up and, following a series of rough interrogations, he was finally shipped over to a prison camp at Sulmona in Italy.

Not very happy at being confined in an Italian prison camp, he was quite naturally delighted when, in September 1943, the Italians finally capitulated. Jerry, quick as always to consolidate in an emergency, sent in an assortment of troops to stem the tide of ex-prisoners now gleefully exploiting their new-found freedom made available when the Italians surrendered all control of the prison camps. Lofty, never a one to look a gift horse in the mouth, immediately took to his heels and scarpered free as a bird in the direction of the open countryside.

Fortune continued for some while to smile upon him. He encountered a group of newly-formed partisans who, in exchange for his expertise in demolition, provided him with food and shelter, until unfortunately at sometime early in the New Year of 1944 during a surprise search carried out by the Jerries, Lofty found himself yet again on the wrong side of the wire.

We were quick to learn that this camp, Stalag 344, wasn't going to be a picnic party. It was being run on unnecessarily strict lines, although with the long days of summer we were able to move around the camp completely unrestricted until the hours of darkness. That did help to break the monotony of lying around on a bunk bed listening to often repeated reminiscences of satisfying meals regrettably long since past. The food in this camp was of an unusually low standard. We argued, sulked and sometimes even fought in the belief that another prisoner had somehow managed to gain an advantage over another by as little perhaps of a few odd grammes of bread.

Morale just wasn't good. I remember there was a huge black water tank used as an emergency supply in the event of a fire and, true or false, I do not know, but it was said that several suicides by drowning had taken place there. Such was the unhappy state there that, although uncertain as to our future, we were delighted to learn that yet again we were to be moved on. In quick succession we were to be given the good and the bad news, the good news being that we were to be sent off with one food parcel between two men, whilst the bad news was that the canned food would once more have the top pierced which again meant that we would not be able to save any of it for very long. We had been strip searched, dusted down with louse powder and, quickly following on the puncturing of our canned food, we were whisked away accompanied as ever by a multitude of constantly screaming half-witted guards to the rail sidings.

CHAPTER SIX

Klimontow (Arbeitskommando)
The language of love

After the dubious joys of the cattle wagon system of rail transport which had so far been our lot, the unexpected arrival at the train siding of a normal civilian, if terribly outdated train, with separate compartments each holding about eight prisoners and one guard, all of whom were perched in comparative luxury along the wooden seats, was to us the absolute ultimate.

Our party, possibly twenty to thirty strong, had left Lamsdorf comforted by the knowledge that, with no advance rations having been issued, our next destination was, in German terms, relatively close. Gazing out in wonderment at the moving scenery of pastoral Deutschland amazed in turn at the slow pace of life in the fields and the urgent frenetic activity centering around the small industrial towns, we made our way eastwards.

The rather sombre, stupid-looking guard allocated to our small party, fidgeting in his ill-fitting uniform and clutching his rifle as a mother, sensing uncertainty or worse, would clutch her child to her bosom, was reluctant to respond to the questioning of a German speaking member of our group. However, under persistent pressure to name our final destination, he grudgingly muttered that we were to journey a matter of a further forty or so miles which would take us to Sosnowitz in Poland and that from there we were to march a few miles further to an Arbeitskommando situated near a coal mine close to the mining village of Klimontow. This information was scarcely the type of news designed to have us leaping up and down in our seats but, as we had many times discovered, being a prisoner meant having absolutely no say in one's destiny.

For the duration of our journey, possibly five hours or so to cover perhaps fifty miles, we had been carefully segregated from the civilian passengers who, apart from a casual glance as they boarded or alighted from the train, had kept at a respectable distance. We had pulled into sidings on numerous occasions to allow the passage of many trains carrying not only troops but several moving at high speed with their flat-bottomed wagons bearing tanks and guns urgently towards the Eastern Front. Passing more slowly and heading for the heart of the homeland were quite a few hospital trains with each carriage surprisingly displaying a huge Red Cross against a square white background. I say surprisingly because the Russians, who were not signatories to the Geneva Convention, didn't acknowledge the existence of the Red Cross Association and therefore would be most unlikely to grant safe conduct to a German train carrying wounded servicemen.

Germany, we felt, was dying, but it was apparently still the expected norm to die in a blaze of glory. Heavy Germanic classical music was borishly blasted out at every opportunity, no stone was left unturned. Music was used to either soothe or stimulate and, as we were later to discover, the radio was mainly used at this critical stage of the war to warn of impending air attacks by the marauding squadrons of allied aircraft seeking to destroy the few remaining industrial targets still unaccountably surviving these onslaughts. This feature stimulated some considerable excitement as the commentary started immediately the bombers entered German air space and continued with a dull monotony not only giving the number of actual 'Terror Flieges' in the attacking force, but also a full uncensored report naming towns and cities that the aircraft were flying over. To us the commentary seemed very similar to the pre-war radio broadcast of the Grand National.

Whatever adversely affected Germany was, of course, a source of great satisfaction to us and it was only when we observed at first hand the horrific shooting down of several of our aircraft that we realised the enormously high cost that was being paid in order to bring the war to its close. Thinking and daydreaming helped to while away the time spent travelling but we were rapidly jolted back to reality on our arrival at Sosnowitz station. As stations go, this we felt, was the absolute ultimate. Huge crowds thronged the heavily-congested platforms: soldiers, sailors, civilians and military police, all of whom seemed to push forward towards the very edge of the platform even before our train had ground to a halt. Getting off, I remember, required a great deal of physical effort and concentration and unfortunately the thought of escaping and losing oneself in the crowd came too late to act on.

Several Polish civilians, shabbily dressed, stood around in small groups and one particular, very elderly lady, dressed from head to foot in black, stepped forward and smilingly gesturing with her right hand held aloft, gave us a 'V' sign. This action caused several of us to respond but our good humour rapidly changed first to shock and then quicker still to helpless rage. A black-clad officer belonging either to a tank regiment or, as we suspected at the time, a full-blown member of the S.S., had rushed over towards the old lady and, with his gloved hand, smacked her full in the face. This assault took place in front of a huge gathering and it was plain to see that many ordinary German soldiers standing around at that time were as appalled as we were. The last view we had of this incident was of this dear old lady being helped to her feet by a number of Polish civilians and although still quite groggy and bloody, I should imagine that it would take much more than a single blow to quell the instincts of people like her.

Our small party was quickly moved away from the station and on towards the centre of this drab industrial town. Along the pavements the Germans strutted and the Poles, obsequiously shuffling along, gave way to them whilst others, clattering along noisily in their wooden-soled footwear, scarcely gave us a glance.

Banners, flags, large posters exhorting a higher degree of help in order to finish the war and smaller printed notices spelling out the dire consequence likely to be suffered by anyone infringing a multitude of alien laws were prolific.

Trams screeching along an agonised path were a further revelation of the conquerors' vindictive demands. Each tram had a separate entrance with a sign clearly reading, 'Nur für Deutsch' whilst a second entrance had yet another notice which proclaimed that as being, 'Für Polen', in other words, maximum segregation from the Master race. Anxious to shake the dust of this unhappy town from our feet, our pace had noticeably increased almost as though by common consent we had all decided that anything in excess of the time we had so far spent here would be a little more than one would wish for.

Across a desolate stretch of wasteland we moved until we finally hit on the small mining village of Klimontow which, if one cares to think about it, spelt backwards reads, 'Wot no milk'. Up to this moment in time I had scarcely given a thought to the fact that Central Europeans, such as the Poles, may not be particularly endowed with our sense of humour but, however, in this respect I would have been sadly mistaken. We had made our way through the main dingy thoroughfare of this grimy little village when lo and behold over on our right hand side we espied a butcher's shop immaculate in appearance with its gleaming steel meat bars and hooks, its marble shelves and three pure white enamelled trays. The whole thing looked terribly inviting but with the long prevailing shortage of meat, the shop was bare. However, and there lies the subtlety of it, the centre tray bore a huge coloured photograph of the Führer whilst the two trays, one on either side, held huge wax pig's heads. The Germans had quite obviously failed to realise the true significance of this humorous display. No marks to the Hun but full marks to Poland's durability.

Shortly after this we began to pick our way through a narrow lane which led directly to a small securely wired compound which, situated adjacent to the coalmine, was to become our place of residence for the foreseeable future.

It was a small camp with possibly six or seven huts, and a smaller hut apparently reserved for the one British prisoner serving a dual function as clerk and interpreter and also for the senior British N.C.O. inappropriately, I felt, known as our 'Man of Confidence'. I personally don't know who he was, I never ever saw him, perhaps it could be that he was too confidential to be seen. These N.C.O.s, unlike ourselves, were volunteers, and it was always our strong belief that they were encouraged out of retirement in the main Stalags by what they considered might be an alleviation of their own living standards rather than to negotiate improved standards for us. The guards' quarters were situated just beyond the wire and close to the main gate and our informants were quick to tell us that the camp Führer was a complete raging nutcase. We lightheartedly accepted this dire snippet of information as we were warmly greeted by many other inmates. Lofty and I struck lucky. We were told that there was accommodation in a particular hut for two other people and it was there that we took our chance.

Amongst those waiting to welcome us was 'Jock' or Alec, Ron Starling, Curly Watts, an Englishman who had served with the Welsh Guards, Danny Miers and several others whose names I have regrettably forgotten. They turned out to be a great crowd and because of this, our stay at Klimontow was a very happy one. We soon became a part of this hut and, apart from the work, which we didn't like, the evenings were times to look forward to.

Fortunately we were at last able to receive first hand news of the Normandy Invasion. The chaps in the hut next to ours had somehow contrived to obtain a radio and, as was customary in these circumstances, no questions were asked. The radio, we gathered, was most probably hidden under the floorboards and brought out only at the hour designated to receive the news via the European Service. This was a great booster to our morale, particularly so after the vastly conflicting items of news put out by Jerry. His news unfailingly served as an almost complete reversal of the B.B.C. news and many times, even though we tried to laugh it off, the reports of our armies being pushed back into the sea were reported with such glib sincerity as to make one believe – such is the power of propaganda. Also present in the hut which housed the illicit radio was an unusually strange character, a white Russian, blond and very tall and handsome, who had somehow managed to survive the unwelcome attention of the Germans – who as we were all too well aware, were rabidly anti-ruski – by assuming the identity of a South African. His English was almost impeccable apart from a slightly clipped accent which could, after all, pass for that of an Afrikaans-speaking colonial. Such was the solidarity of the inmates of this chap that although each and every one of us was aware of the radio and of the true identity of 'Jan', no one spoke out of turn.

On one occasion when we returned from our labours, we were surprised to each find on our bed a printed copy of a leaflet in English which, I remember, was headed 'To all prisoners of war. The escape from prison camps is no longer a sport', and went on to list the diabolical penalties likely to befall anyone who might be tempted to 'Zurück laufen', or as it was most commonly put, 'walk back'.

Air raids in this neck of the woods were becoming more frequent and intensive than any previously experienced. We had, by the gracious permission of the Third Reich, a rather

large and deep 'Luftschutz Raum' laboriously excavated by
former inmates of the camp and when the bombers came too
close for comfort, we were unceremoniously herded below
ground where we would languish in idle safety until the raid
had passed. This part of Poland and also certain areas of the
more easterly parts of Silesia were heavily industrialised and
so far as air raids were concerned they had been particularly
fortunate. However, now, and indeed for several months past,
their luck had changed.

A short spell of work in the coal mine had proved, at least
from the German point of view, completely unproductive and,
after a very necessary reorganisation of labour, we found ourselves transferred en masse to a nearby sand quarry. The work
down the mine had been, to say the least, both dangerous and
boring. It had been said that since this mine was declared free
of all gases, it was necessary, or so they said, to be equipped
with a small carbide lamp with an exposed flame which didn't
somehow seem right. It was manned mainly by Polish civilian
miners and supervised by a mixture of ethnic German officials and, very much lower down the scale, a tasty bunch of
in-betweens known as Volksdeutsch, a not-too-comely bunch
of Poles brought within the warm embrace of the Third Reich
and honoured with a form of second-class citizenship. The
mine was terribly outdated and this situation, coupled with
its reluctant group of forced labourers, had gradually reduced
the output of coal to an abysmal all time low. Hence our
permanent and rapid transfer to pastures new. The situation in
the sand quarry to which we were consigned was an altogether
different one. However, not being particularly interested in
either the functioning or the mal-functioning of the coal
industry in general and in particular the German side of the
business, we never 'knowingly aided or abetted their cause'.
It was a great improvement being able to go through the
motions of working in the open air even though the hours
were terribly long. We were expected to work seven days a
week from around 7 a.m. until around 5 p.m. with a mid-day
break of half an hour and with one Sunday off in four weeks.
Looking at the quarry for the first time, it reminded me of a
moon crater. It was of a tremendous circumference and with
a possible depth of fifteen to twenty feet. A single sentry
box-type toilet was situated smack in the middle of the quarry
and it was always the golden rule that one must seek the

permission of a guard before leaving one's work station to use a toilet. As in the coal mine, the main labour force was again Polish and Volksdeutsch whilst we endeavoured without skill or enthusiasm, to emulate the time-wasting tactics of the more experienced and crafty Poles.

Sand was dug out of the quarry and loaded into metal skips which were later coupled together on a narrow gauge railway line and finally hauled to the coal mine by a small, ancient and almost completely expired steam engine driven, we were quick to note, by a very attractive Polish girl with pleasant features, long dark hair and dressed in an uncomplimentary ill-fitting boiler suit. Maybe in retrospect she wasn't as eye-catching as we thought but bearing in mind the fact that this was the first female we had met at close quarters for many a long month, she certainly looked the cat's whiskers. Summer, by this time, was rapidly drawing to a close and although the poor quality German food had been infrequently supplemented by the odd Red Cross food parcel, the chill winds of early autumn had renewed our desire to stock up a little more food for what could be a long, hard winter. Working close to the Poles meant that from time to time, and assuming that one had something with which to barter, one could always obtain that odd item of luxury such as an egg or possibly a half loaf of bread.

Lofty and I had occasionally ventured into this black market situation exchanging the odd pair of socks (Lofty's) or perhaps the odd packet of rock hard inedible prunes (mine – courtesy of the Red Cross) and, on this fateful occasion, the sacrificial and major offering chanced to be an old and threadbare pullover donated albeit begrudgingly by Lofty.

We had, by what was the accepted norm, conducted negotiations unobserved by our guards and with painstaking care managed to convey by sign language our need to obtain bread in exchange for this time-expired pullover. The Pole we were bartering with had, by dint of exhaustive gesticulations and a smattering of German and Polish jumble, agreed to let us have, on the following day, a whole one and a half kilo loaf in exchange for the pullover.

We accepted this and on the following morning we quietly made contact with the Pole who, although still eager to carry out the transaction, seemed quite nervous and agitated. He assured us that the promised loaf was to hand and that it was at that particular moment in time carefully hidden aboard the steam engine driven by the young girl we had noticed before and who now turned out to be his daughter! The cunning old whatsit had obviously opted out of the transaction feeling far too twitchy to take the risk himself, and had passed the buck and the risk over to his daughter.

An agreement was reached on the understanding that, at a given signal from him, either Lofty or myself would seek permission to visit the solitary toilet which stood on a levelled piece of ground in the centre of the quarry. At the same time, his daughter, the engine driver, would leave her engine and move across towards the rear of the toilet with the bread and the exchange would take place quickly and without fuss. Lofty, who owned the pullover, had automatically elevated himself to a position as the founder of the feast and was quick off the mark to nominate me as the one to do the actual swopping. On a signal from the Pole who had now noticed his daughter moving over towards the rear of the toilet, I immediately sought permission from the nearest guard to visit the toilet.

All would no doubt have gone well but, totally indignant to discover that the girl had been given only half the quantity of bread agreed, I doggedly refused to hand over Lofty's pullover. Whilst this problem was taking my full attention I had failed to notice a very excited Lofty who had charged over to warn me that the girl and I had been spotted by two guards who were even now moving over towards us.

Unable to dodge them, we were caught red-handed and, as was custom and practice for any offence, our identity discs were snatched from around our necks. We never did find out what happened to the girl. In fact the only clue as to her predicament lay in the belief that as she never again surfaced in that neck of the woods, she had become amongst other things either a transferred or redundant engine driver. I'm not being unkind towards her, neither am I suggesting that anything particularly unpleasant may have happened to her − she was most probably transferred to another work site whilst on the other hand we, on our return from our labours, were immediately fallen upon and taken to attend at the office of the unpredictable Feldwebel of whom we had heard so much since our arrival here. He was, or so it was said, the ex-heavyweight boxing champion of Silesia who had been medically retired from the ring after a number of unsuccessful bouts which had reduced him to a state little short of being totally punch drunk. Came the war, and, following a particularly nasty clash with a bunch of obstinate Russian gunners, his active career ended with a piece of shrapnel in his skull.

Such therefore was the condition of the human time bomb we were now destined to encounter. Ushered into his presence, Lofty and I, accompanied by the two guards witness to our present problem and the camp interpreter, glanced down at the Feldwebel's desk where he sat silently weighing us up and at the same time beating a noisy tattoo on the table top with our identity discs, one in either hand. Speaking rapidly in an agitated manner, he gradually and in a frenzy of rage began to work up to an ear-piercing climax which scarcely gave time for the interpreter to translate – it was only then that we, finally seeing the light of day, came to accept the term 'a captive audience'. However, having temporarily exhausted himself, the camp interpreter somehow managed to explain the charge levelled against us. What an incredibly strange mind this character had, he was actually charging us with the 'attempted seduction of a German subject'. Our immediate reaction was to laugh. Did he not realise, we said, that under-nourished prisoners such as ourselves had, literally speaking, absolutely no interest whatsoever in the female presence even to the point of embracing the most attractive mädchen in or out of circulation? Obviously not. However, he paused long enough to allow for a further response and Lofty, never slow to offer reason, replied in a conciliatory tone asking the Feldwebel how a charge of that nature could possibly be substantiated when it was known that neither of us spoke a single word of Polish. A rabid darkening of our accuser's brow heralded the screaming outburst that was to follow as, with an explicitly rude gesture with his fingers, he mouthed a reply which was equally graphically translated by the interpreter to the effect that, 'The language of love is universal' – hence, no need for conversation in Polish or any other language!

Our punishment, trivial and petty as it may seem, was to be made to stand to attention for two hours each night on our return from work outside the gate and under the gaze of a niggling guard delegated, albeit unwillingly, to perform this extra turn of duty.

The boys in our hut were particularly good and somehow always managed to keep our soup hot until we were allowed back inside. From time to time our little charmer, the Feldwebel, would circulate around the inside of the camp seeking to uncover whatever heinous crime was being perpetrated within his kingdom.

Outside the wire he was persecuting the guards, most of whom, elderly or disabled, were beginning to live in dread of his paranoic outbursts. He would rouse all off-duty guards, load them up with gear and pack them off, singing as they marched all the morale-lifting marching songs of former years including a regular rendition of an early 1940 popular tune which had long since lost its footing on the Top of the Pops – 'Wir Marschieren Gegen England'. This, thought some of the chaps, was a form of poetic justice since, in the early days of the war which as we all know almost concluded in a disastrous defeat after Dunkirk, the Germans, cock-a-hoop with confidence had, in certain prison camps, withheld food until the prisoners had sung several encores of a song that at one time had been very popular in England, 'We're going to hang out the washing on the Siegfried Line'. Now, hearing these worn out, jaded and exhausted guardians of the Third Reich being made to look foolish was, to the veteran prisoners of Dunkirk, highly amusing.

Shortly after our brief encounter with the Polish civilians, we were relieved of our, 'highly skilled', task of loading sand and, dare I say it, elevated to the task of loading huge pre-cast sections of concrete sewer pipes on small flat-bottomed trucks, pushing them some distance and unloading on to a stockpile. The object of the exercise was to transport as many as possible as gently as possible but, with only two guards plus two Volksdeutsch overseers to control us, it must be admitted with great regret that a very high percentage of sewer pipes were accidentally smashed due, I suppose, to 'careless handling'.

At this time, late Autumn, the weather had most certainly taken a turn for the worse competing at times, we thought, with the moods of our Feldwebel. Our two-tier bunk beds had begun to suffer due to the unexpectedly sharp drop in temperature as our straw-filled mattress was supported by six short lengths of wood which extended across the width of the bunk. Notwithstanding the fact that we were living adjacent to a coalmine, we were hard pressed to come up with the means of keeping warm, and therefore, in fair and strict rotation, we gradually burnt up most of our bed boards which left

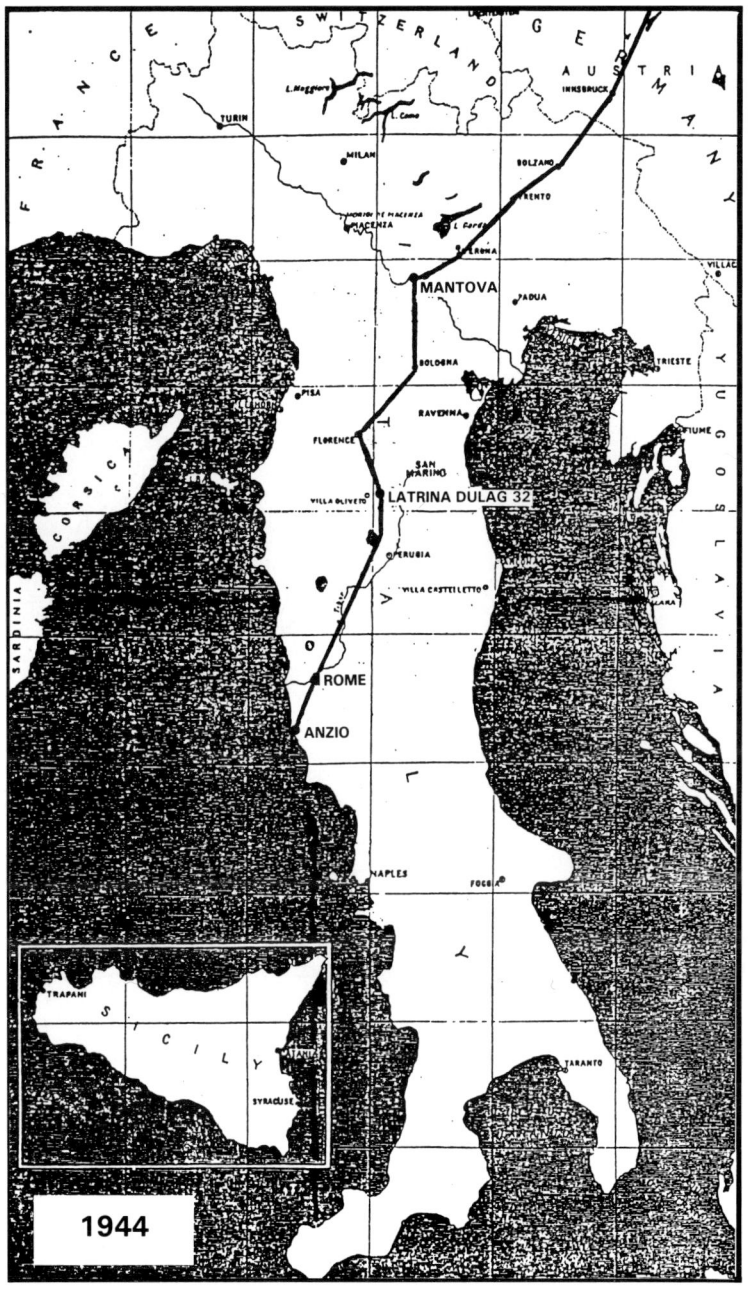

My road to Germany from Anzio through the Brenner Pass and onwards to Austria.

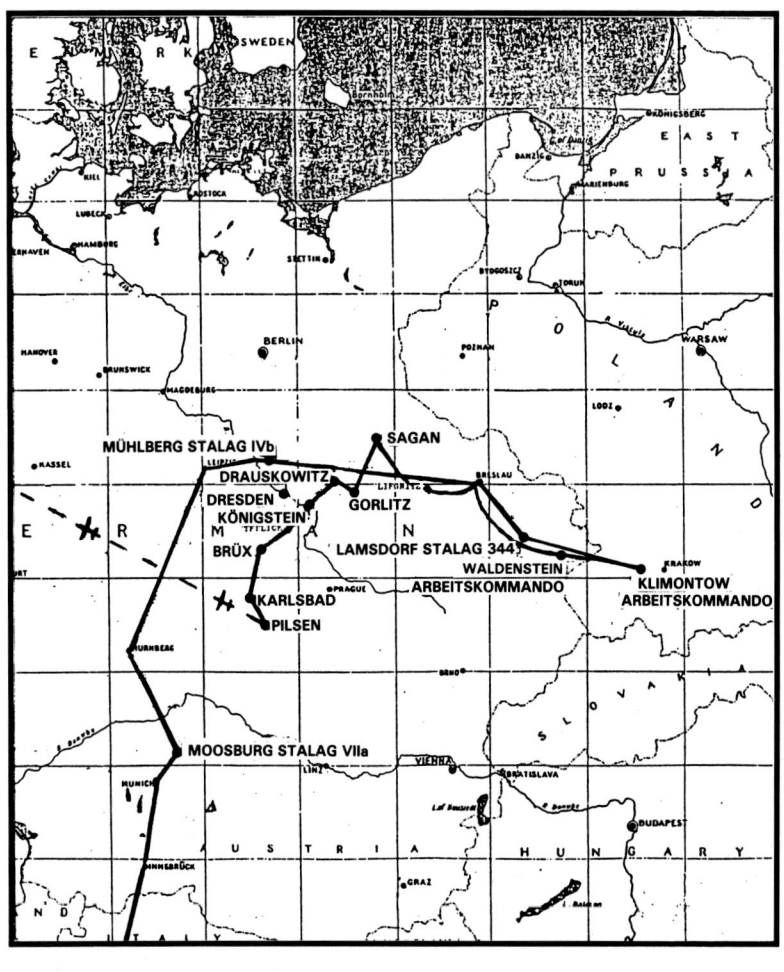

My route through Austria, Germany, Poland and Czechoslovakia and finally by air to the U.K.

As a result of repeated applications from British subjects from all parts of the world wishing to take part in the common European struggle against Bolshevism authorisation has recently been given for the creation of a British volunteer unit.

The British Free Corps publishes herewith the following short statement of the aims and principles of the unit.

1) The British Free Corps is a thoroughly British volunteer unit, conceived and created by British subjects from all parts of the Empire who have taken up arms and pledged their lives in the common European struggle against Soviet Russia.

2) The British Free Corps condemns the war with Germany and the sacrifice of British blood in the interests of Jewry and International Finance, and regards this conflict as a fundamental betrayal of the British People and British Imperial interests.

3) The British Free Corps desires the establishment of peace in Europe, the development of close friendly relations between England and Germany, and the encouragement of mutual understanding and collaboration between the two great Germanic peoples.

4) The British Free Corps will neither make war against Britain or the British Crown, nor support any action or policy detrimental to the interests of the British People.

Published by the British Free Corps

Copy of a pamphlet circulated by the Germans during my stay in Stalag VIIa (Moosburg).

Stalag VIIIb (344). Translated from the Polish: 'Monument of Fascism victims in Lambinowice, erected in memory of the murdered prisoners of war in Wermachts camps, Lamsdorf'.

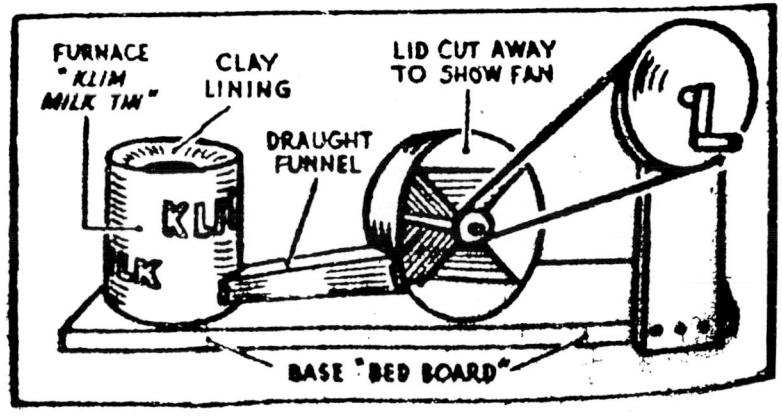

The 'Blower'.

Tom (Lofty) Banks, Royal Engineers.

To all Prisoners of War!

The escape from prison camps is no longer a sport!

Germany has always kept to the Hague Convention and only punished recaptured prisoners of war with minor disciplinary punishment.

Germany will still maintain these principles of international law.

But England has besides fighting at the front in an honest manner instituted an illegal warfare in non combat zones in the form of gangster commandos, terror bandits and sabotage troops even up to the frontiers of Germany.

They say in a captured secret and confidential English military pamphlet,

THE HANDBOOK
OF MODERN IRREGULAR
WARFARE:

". . . the days when we could practise the rules of sportsmanship are over. For the time being, every soldier must be a potential gangster and must be prepared to adopt their methods whenever necessary."

"The sphere of operations should always include the enemy's own country, any occupied territory, and in certain circumstances, such neutral countries as he is using as a source of supply."

England has with these instructions opened up a non military form of gangster war!

Germany is determined to safeguard her homeland, and especially her war industry and provisional centres for the fighting fronts. Therefore it has become necessary to create strictly forbidden zones, called death zones, in which all unauthorised trespassers will be immediately shot on sight.

Escaping prisoners of war, entering such death zones, will certainly lose their lives. They are therefore in constant danger of being mistaken for enemy agents or sabotage groups.

Urgent warning is given against making future escapes!

In plain English: Stay in the camp where you will be safe! Breaking out of it is now a damned dangerous act.

The chances of preserving your life are almost nil!

All police and military guards have been given the most strict orders to shoot on sight all suspected persons.

Escaping from prison camps has ceased to be a sport!

Copy of a pamphlet issued to all prisoners during my stay at the Arbeitskommando (Klimontow, Poland).

Bill Pedersen visiting Jack's grave at Charlottenburg cemetery in Berlin, 1988.

Jack Pedersen, 24 Battalion, N.Z. Infantry.

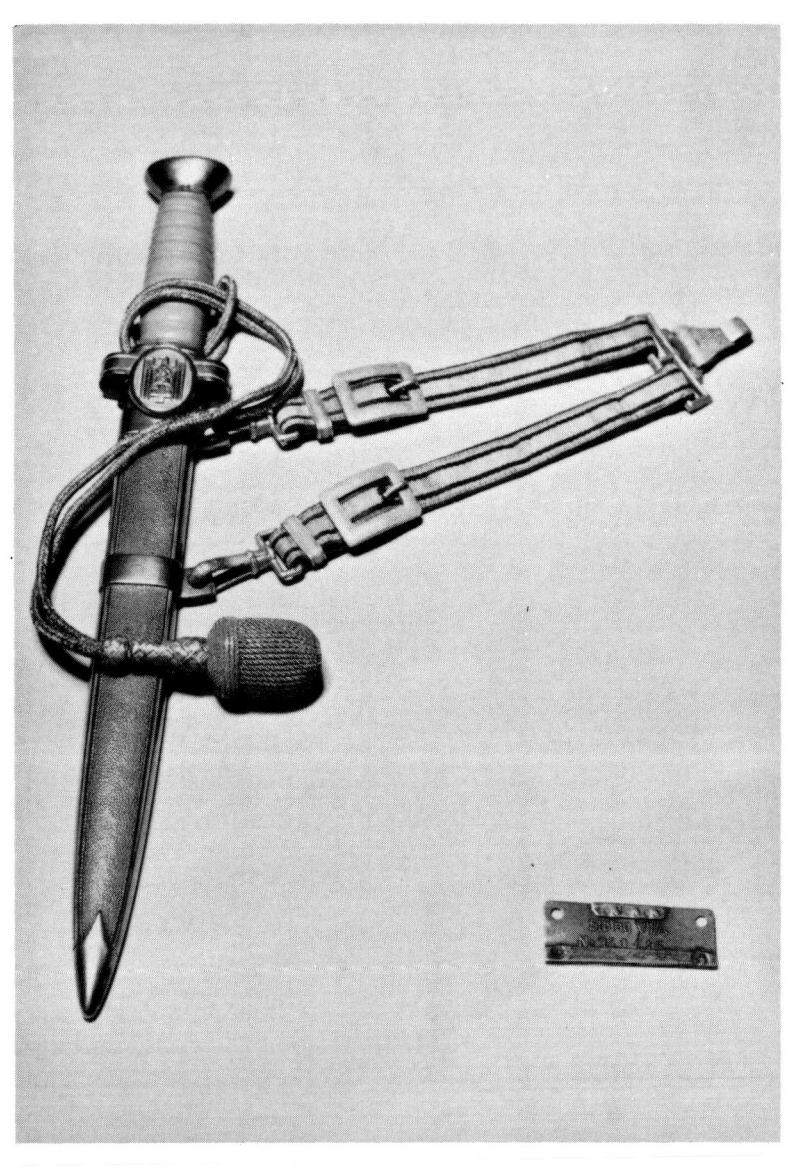

ABOVE: *Nazi Dress Bayonet, given to the author by the Bürgomeister of Brüx, Czechoslovakia, May 1945.*
ABOVE RIGHT: *Surviving half of the author's Stalag identity disc.*

us at night precariously balanced on three boards per man with one board each at our head and feet and with a totally inadequate third board propping up our middle section. We joked about it, we cursed it, but we did, I suppose, extract a minimal amount of warmth from our sacrifice and on a particularly memorable evening we had reached an unusually low threshold of boredom. The gramophone – a record player to the uninformed – which circulated around the different huts on a weekly loan basis, had recently passed out of our hands. It was a decrepit object, hand cranked and boasting a broken sewing needle in place of a stylus. The sound reproduction was woefully grim but it didn't really matter because the only record we had was an almost inaudible rendition of the 'Pennsylvania Polka'.

Such was the state of affairs which initially prompted the exchange of a few yarns, supported at a later stage by a few funny stories and a bit of a sing-song. I'm sure it was never intended – it was almost certainly unrehearsed – but we found ourselves singing a derisory and frankly bawdy version of the German National Anthem, 'Deutschland Über Alles'. This, unfortunately, prompted an immediate response in the shape of our resident host, the Feldwebel who, hammering on the door, screamed for silence. We quietened down for a while but, out of sheer devilment once he had left, we struck up again, this time, if possible, a wee bit more vociferous than before.

A sudden crash against the door accompanied by a series of thoughtfully selected Germanic oaths and the excited barking of the guard dogs straining at the leash and baying for our blood was a little too much to take in at such short notice as, with trembling hands, the hut door was clumsily unlocked and in charged our demented Feldwebel, a whole gaggle of guards and two huge hostile anti-British alsatians.

Panic followed: the guards hit out with their rifle butts, the dogs snapped and snarled, taking samples of flesh at will and we, having now overcome our original surprise and ensuing panic had joyfully settled down to an agreeably amusing end-of-an-evening session.

The guards, and even in fact the Feldwebel, had now begun to falter. The excitement had been just too much for them to cope with. Voices were noticeably weaker than before. The dogs continued to snap and barks although admittedly in a less enthusiastic manner than at the beginning and we, having sought refuge along the higher reaches of the upper bunk beds had discovered, much to our alarm, that the three remaining bed boards supporting each mattress had long since lost any value so far as supporting the weight of several prisoners desperately anxious to avoid the fangs of these hungry, excited and very anti-social dogs. Not too long afterwards and to our crowning delight the whole fiasco collapsed into a stalemate almost as quickly as it had started. The Sheriff of Klimontow had withdrawn his merry men and the dogs, now far too exhausted to be anything but abjectly fawning and friendly, were lured away after several fond and affectionate farewells. In fact they had become so fond of us that, with a final gesture of ever-lasting friendship, one of the brutes actually pissed on Lofty's leg.

CHAPTER SEVEN

Klimontow

That unwanted feeling

Klimontow, thanks to the supportive attitude of the inmates was, on the whole, a very good camp. Shortages of food, petty restrictions and long working hours were carelessly shrugged off against a background of solidarity. We had many lighthearted moments, many at the expense of the Jerry who, on so many occasions, became the butt of our humour. Take Danny as an example or, to give him his full title, Daniel Mears. The name sounded suspiciously Jewish and Danny, with a shock of jet black hair, swarthy features and an abundance of nasal architecture, was sufficiently suspect to become a natural target for the guards who would, with their sick sense of humour, load on him all the petty, irksome and dirty jobs around the camp. But being an exceptionally mild-mannered chap, he had so far remained quite philosophical about it all. However, as with all things human, there comes a breaking point and Danny, as British as a bacon butty, was about to make his stand.

It happened, I remember, during an evening roll call that had taxed the mathematical prowess of the guards a little more mentally than usual. To me, it was always a mystery as to why the Germans, unable to count in fives, would always insist in arranging us in ranks of five for the sake of simplicity because, figuratively speaking, it just didn't add up. They always got flustered and the more flustered they became then the more aggressive they felt. Slow-witted to a man and, in actual fact, very similar to a bull being provoked, the Germans' inability to conduct a simple count enraged them to the point where we deputised as a red rag to these angry and baffled bulls.

Frustration had also crept in on our side as we felt, quite rightly, that things had gone far beyond an acceptable limit and, amidst a string of insults and, by now complete non-co-operation, the Jerry was getting more rattled than ever.

Yet another re-count was started, this time calling out in fives and, in a desperate attempt to somehow get it right, the counting Jerry would touch the front man in every five on the shoulder.

Approaching Danny, who most likely muttered some uncomplimentary remark, the guard responded with a sharp jab directed at Danny's shoulder, at the same time calling out 'Jude'. This, aggravated by the long frustrating waiting about on the roll call finally brought this tedious business to an unexpected climax when Danny, balefully glaring at the offending guard, slowly and deliberately unbuckled the belt supporting his trousers. His next move was to unbutton his flies and slowly lower his trousers which now revealed a pair of grey 'long john' type underpants which stretched from his waist right down to the ankles. By this time a hush had descended on the entire assembly. The guards, the interpreter and the Feldwebel, all of whom were gazing in wonderment at Danny's performance and possibly fearful of the danger of a full-scale riot, were completely taken back by the final move which finished up with the 'long johns' now released and lying collapsed in concertina fashion round Danny's ankles whilst he, standing half naked and in all his glory, pointed to his very personal possessions and ground out a question aimed at the assembled Jerries, 'Have you ever seen a Jew with a foreskin like this?'.

The Germans were utterly spellbound, the camp dolmetscher, struggling to interpret the question posed by Danny, seemed for once to be at a loss for words, the Feldwebel moved forward for a closer inspection and the initial problem regarding the unhappy counting of heads had been forgotten.

Facts are facts no matter where one is and the fact in this case was made abundantly clear by Danny who, it must be said, was never again called on to perform and to prove his national identity.

Over the weeks following our encounter at the roll call, we had several small diversions. We were paid our wages in what was commonly known as 'Lager Geld' – camp money – and what a completely useless exercise that was. There was nothing to spend it on other than buying a couple of packets of Pudding Pulvers, very similar to a blancmange mixed with water and devoid of any recognisable flavour. We were each given a postcard to send to our next-of-kin with pre-printed messages which read something like, 'I'm well/I'm not well' etc., leaving us to delete as necessary. This was to be my only direct written communication with home and, owing to the unhealthy state of the German transport system which had more or less been bombed out of existence, I was never fortunate enough to receive a message in return.

Out of sheer boredom, I'd reported for dental treatment and, in the company of two other prisoners, managed a trip out to visit a Polish dentist in Sosnowitz. Our guard insisted on all of us sitting on the floor in the shabbily-equipped dental surgery where we were each in turn able to witness the agonies of primitive dentistry being inflicted by an enthusiastic but terribly unskilled dentist.

I'm certain I didn't need any treatment, I only went along for an inspection and a walk but that didn't in any way convince the dentist who seemed quite anxiously concerned to keep on the right side of the Master Race. He filled a tooth using a manual, treadle-operated drilling machine, in a fashion which made me wonder if perhaps he'd kept my head revolving around a stationary drill rather than the other way round. Local anaesthetics, nowadays freely administered, were never given to alleviate pain during the filling of a tooth and even the luxury of a high speed drill was never on offer.

So much, however for that, my first and last incursion into dental malingering. Had I but known that a further trip had been planned to take in the delights of that very drab and unhappy town, Sosnowitz, I would no doubt have fared better as a member of a team of 'volunteers' who had been ordered to carry out a so far unspecified labour of love in that town. The group had been taken into Sosnowitz and were surprised to be escorted directly into the local Nazi Party Headquarters where it was explained to them that they must bodily lift and carry down a very narrow flights of stairs a huge safe which, by all accounts, weighed something in the region of half a ton. This was understandably a mammoth task for undernourished prisoners to carry out. Apart from the enormous weight involved, no consideration had been given to the narrow width of the staircase which seemed to totally cancel out the physical handling of this cumbersome object.

More important still, however, was the negative approach to anything even faintly related to work and this we were told was to end in a complete fiasco. A council of war between the guards and a few minor party officials produced little in the way of a solution. The prisoners, squatting on their haunches, were refusing to attempt to move the safe and, sensing an advantage, had demanded liquid refreshment which, to the amazement of all concerned, resulted in the offer by the Germans of a small keg of ersatz beer. A further demand, this time for food, was a wee bit too much for the Jerries who, strengthening their resistance to the blackmail attempts, refused any further concessions and openly threatened to keep the prisoners there until the job was done.

This threat may well have been the undoing of the entire operation as the ringleader, now cunningly pretending to capitulate, gave in and asked for a long length of stout rope and, after a tedious search, this was found and hastily handed to the prisoners.

By a concerted effort, the safe was half dragged and half slid along through the door and onto the top of the staircase. The rope was looped around this heavy object and then allowed, quite gently, to be lowered so slowly and so gently with the prisoners in a tug-of-war position steadying its descent by acting in unison, until, on a pre-arranged signal, the rope was abruptly released and the safe tumbled headlong down the stairs and finally crashed to a shuddering halt on the landing below, bringing half the wall down with it. The happy band of prisoners, fortified with a minor victory and a bladder full of saccharin-sweetened ersatz beer, were unceremoniously chased back to the place from whence they had so recently come!

One other character of note was a Pole recently elevated to the ranks of the co-operative Volksdeutsch. An ugly brute of a man, he was mishapen both in mind and body and with a head so huge as to prompt one to wonder how on earth it could be supported on his narrow sloping shoulders. If anything could possibly compete with his nasty unwholesome appearance then some credit must be allowed in respect of his temper. Not only did his flat-faced features reflect a minimal degree of animal-like cunning but, when those close-set eyes began to twitch, then that was the time to back off.

He was an armed civilian, quick to take offence and as officious and ingratiating towards the Germans as to make one want to vomit. For many weeks we had been blessed with his company whilst out on work parties and, with great satisfaction, we had taken to addressing him, complete with a click of the heels, as 'Herr Bighead'.

Now until a certain day, he had literally wallowed in the ingratiating servile respect which the Engländers were apparently bestowing on him. We sought the advice of 'Herr Bighead', we politely requested 'Herr Bighead's' permission to use the toilet. Such was the mentality of the man that he had fallen for our mickey-taking hook, line and sinker. However, as all good things come to an end, so did our fun and games.

Some kill-joy Jerry enlightened him as to the true meaning of his much cherished title and the first prisoner to approach him on that day had need to duck rapidly to avoid a skull-crushing swipe delivered via the butt of our late 'friend's' rifle.

Our time spent at Klimontow had been a relatively happy time. Granted, food had been in short supply, the weather now in early November had turned decidedly uncharitable and the amount of work that was being demanded of us began to reach unacceptable heights. But to completely offset these shortcomings, it must be said that the spirit of unity that existed within our community was unparalleled. We lived purely on the support of each other, nobody stepped out of line, nobody asked for more than one was able to give. There was no quarrelling, no petty thieving but just a good-natured resolve to stick it out for however long it might be. We certainly knew that the end was approaching but a state of confusion frequently made us doubt the actual speed of the Allied Victory.

For many months now, we had seen the Allied Airforces' planes crossing the sky at will, completely unchallenged by the Luftwaffe. We received daily bulletins via our clandestine radio which usually gave a very optimistic picture of the progress of the invasion which by all accounts had succeeded in crossing the Rhine at several points. On the other hand we had the German propaganda news sheets giving, quite naturally, a completely different story. However, adding to the general confusion of thoughts was a selection of unquestionably authentic photographs of the streets in Aachen littered with the crumpled bodies of Allied servicemen and several other shots of dispirited soldiers late of the 1st Airborne Division being led into captivity after the abortive landings at Arnhem. Little wonder that under these stressful circumstances aggravated by undernourishment and uncertainty, we sometimes found it all a bit too much to swallow. The boot – or could it be the jackboot? – was now on the other foot. In our time we'd conned our superiors, we'd conned Ities, Jerries, Froggies, Gyppos – you name it, we'd conned them.

Propaganda, subterfuge, call it what you may, was, one could almost say, an art we hadn't actually invented but we had practised and worked on it from day one of our service and, at the risk of appearing boastful, suffice to say that we were awfully proficient. The application of confusion in order to create a pecuniary advantage might best describe its application when, on occasions far too numerous to mention, we had supplemented our low service pay by what could, I suppose, be considered 'questionable means'.

Lofty and I had been exchanging notes on this very issue and, not to be outdone, I went on to relate my story regarding an overdose of subterfuge which a colleague and I had inflicted on a vast number of very raw and very gullible American servicemen stationed in Tunis after the end of the African campaign.

Highlighting the issue as to how we bent the truth, I went on to explain that we had somehow managed to 'liberate' a huge wooden case which, on opening, was found to contain a staggeringly large number of cheap plastic encased compasses. Now my friend, 'Gary' Cooper, formerly of Liverpool and an astute entrepreneur to boot, rapidly set about putting together a quick get-rich scheme at the expense of the American servicemen who, at that particular stage of the war, were quite unworldly and terribly susceptible to the devious wiles of we, the more accomplished survivors, and were to become his, or our, unsuspecting victims.

His modus operandi was simple enough to almost bring the tears to my eyes. We made our way to the centre of Tunis where we quickly headed for a huge park which had been taken over as an American vehicle park and there, with pockets and a small canvas sack stuffed to capacity with these cheap compasses, we sat on a vacant park bench and waited for our first lamb to deliver himself to the slaughter.

Gary, a more seasoned campaigner than I, insisted that I should play the stooge and that I should only respond as and when required to do so. Completely mystified and feeling a little self-conscious, I was to watch in amazement when he idly fished out a compass from his copious supply, shook it several times before quizically holding it close to his ear as though hoping to hear it tick.

A few Americans idly strolling by, began slowly but surely to group around us as Gary sat quietly carrying out his well-rehearsed performance with the compass. In an unbelievably short space of time we had quite an appreciable audience and then, for Gary, the expected happened as one intrepid Yank, more pushy than the rest, pushed to the front of the gathering and, in a loud nasal voice, informed Gary that what he was shaking was in fact not a watch but a Goddam German compass. 'Do you,' the American asked, 'want to sell it?'. Gary, faking reluctance to be parted from his new-found treasure, responded with a resounding refusal to even consider the proposal. Now, when an American is faced with a commercially-orientated situation such as this, then the sky becomes the limit and sure enough an escalation of bids rained in from all quarters.

In Tunis the currency was officially French Francs and before long the bidding had reached an absolutely astronomical height before Gary, reluctant as before to part with this increasingly valuable toy, insisted in a loud voice that I should part with mine. None of those assembled suspected, even for a moment, that we had several dozen more waiting to be loaded on them and throughout the day, playing the same silly scene to similar audiences of other gullible Yanks in different parts of this huge vehicle park, screaming to part with their cash, we began to amass a small fortune in exchange for those useless bits of plastic.

The first snow of winter had already descended on us albeit at this stage a mere flurry and in no way indicative of all that was to follow and I suppose in a resigned way we had girded our loins to settle down in Klimontow to a hard and possibly hungry winter but, however, that was not to be. An unexpected order came, to the effect that six of our noble band, including myself, were to attend for an unexpected and unsolicited medical examination.

Sitting in the cramped depressing waiting room awaiting my turn, I was conducting a mental roll call of those present who, like myself, had been selected for this surprise check-up. There was Jock, or Alec, of whom we shall hear much more, we had Ben, a solid and amiable Yorkshireman, two other chaps, Jeff and Ron, who had so far kept very much to themselves and also another chap of whom I remember very little.

Jock was the first to be called into the surgery and on his return some fifteen minutes later, he expressed his opinion of the situation. The doctor, he said, was Polish, totally sympathetic and, by all accounts, very concerned for our welfare. Encouraged by all that he said, I eventually made my way into the surgery full of intent to give the performance of my life.

I was asked in a mixture of Polish, German and broken English to strip off and to indicate, so far as I could, any physical problems I may or may not be suffering from. With a tear-jerking start and beginning at my head, I complained of dizzy spells, sick headaches, earache, eye strain and goodness knows what, so that by the time I had reached the defects in my legs, ankles and feet, he was looking so pitifully impressed that I had a sudden feeling that had I been a horse and he a vet, he would no doubt have had me put down.

Back in the waiting room, dressed and cock-a-hoop with my acting prowess, I felt completely assured that if the powers-that-be didn't repatriate me as a totally disabled person, then at the very least I would most likely become hospitalised. The affront to my esteem can only be judged when we were awakened very early one morning to be packed off without any by-your-leave to work in an even bleaker neck of the woods hewing stone out of a quarry. So much for gullible doctors!

It must have happened at three or perhaps four o'clock in the morning. Those staying behind got up to bid us farewell. Lofty, Curly, Danny and Ron Starling were amongst those staying behind and although terribly short of personal possessions, I remember Jock and I were given an odd assortment of going away gifts such as a sewing needle, a cigarette, a length of string and even a few pages of a well-thumbed novel.

One could scarcely imagine a more dreary and depressing start to a day as, again clutching a rock-hard one hundred gramme ration of black bread thinly spread with ersatz margarine, we made our way through the grey, damp, bitterly cold silence of early morning. The mood of our guards was completely in tune with the atmosphere, they plodded on silently and apart from the occasional grunted refusal of our requests to stop for a break, there was literally no contact between us.

By the time we arrived at Sosnowitz railway station, for that was our immediate destination, daylight had caught up with us and the streets were once again alive with people, in fact apart from the incident involving the old lady on our arrival at this grim-looking station, the whole scene was a pure re-enactment of what we had first encountered. The station boasted a Red Cross refreshment trolley with female volunteers briskly and efficiently dispensing food and drink to the insatiable hoardes of Fritzes thronging the platform but, unfortunately for us anyway, the cupboard was bare.

After what seemed an eternity spent waiting around on this soulless platform, our sluggish, ancient and unheated personenzug finally ground to a halt. We boarded a small compartment where we sat tightly packed with a guard sitting comfortably one on each side of the two wooden bench seats and occupying by an incontestable right far more space than they needed.

We slowly wound our way resolutely and hesitantly halting, it often seemed, to allow the engine to draw breath, at Katowitz, Gliwitz and numerous other small stations in addition to the many unscheduled stops where we frequently languished in comfortless, long-forgotten sidings. Eventually, however, and shortly after passing through Oppeln we came, quite unexpectedly, to the end of our journey when we finally ground to a halt at a small isolated station smack bang in the middle of nowhere.

Alighting with a feeling of oppressive gloom, the flimsy wooden platform creaked in protest at the weight of far more passengers than it had ever catered for. The bleak, open countryside dotted here and there with a few squalid-looking cottages failed to suppress our doubts. Snow, now falling and swirling in a tantalizing fashion, was already beginning to form into drifts as the wind, bitterly cold, began to compound this aura of desolation.

Our party was brought to a halt under the curious dull-eyed gaze of a small knot of villagers who, appearing from nowhere, had gathered to witness our arrival and, just by the sheer luck of the draw, I happened to be standing at the head of the small group which unfortunately meant that when the party was divided off into two sections, I found myself departing in the one direction with Jeff who, I believe, hailed from Nottingham and Ron, an agreeable though taciturn character who, pre-war, ran a small grocery shop in Hull, whilst Jock, Ben and the other chap went shooting off in the other direction.

A short walk quickly brought us to our destination which proved to be a very small well fenced-in enclosure containing a single barrack-type hut with a small washhouse adjoining it. Outside and immediately to the left of the compound stood the guards' quarters which were dwarfed by a huge brick kiln and several ancillary worksheds.

We were met at the gate by the permanent guard commander, the British Man of Confidence, a sergeant who had formerly served with the Green Howards, and a French Canadian Sanitäter on hand to provide our basic medical needs. Nothing concerning any member of our reception committee impressed me sufficiently for me to remember their names. Maybe I'm being a trifle uncharitable in my sentiments but when one bears in mind as I do the back-breaking work in which we were to become involved extracting stone from the quarry in bitterly cold weather with worn out tools whilst at the same time existing on little more than a starvation diet, then one would, I suppose, quite naturally resent the vastly different life enjoyed by our two permanent billet minders.

At around six o'clock in the evening the two work parties returned from their labours. The smaller party came in from the kilns where their task was to feed the ovens for the firing of the stone removed from the quarry. The object of this exercise was never made clear although I believe the stone was used, among other things, to produce one of the basic components needed to make saccharin, a commodity very much in use throughout Germany. This task, although arduous, was in no way as demanding as that of actually working on the quarry face. This point was made absolutely clear to me when I witnessed the return of the second and largest party from their labours. My first impression was that not only were they worn out but also far more withdrawn than our former colleagues back in Klimontow.

These chaps had very little to say. Granted, we were introduced and answered the few questions asked of us but somehow for want of a better description this was not a particularly good atmosphere. Out of the twenty or so inmates of our hut we had an Australian, a chap called Chambers, a sometimes perky little Yorkshireman answering to the name of 'Yorkie', Jimmy − can't remember his surname − who slept on the bunk above mine and the most unforgettable of those present, a New Zealander, Jack Pedersen.

The evenings here were dull with conversation of an interesting nature strictly limited in content. We were, I suppose, a small ill-matched group thrown together by circumstance and greatly inhibited by the problems which beset us, and I had the feeling that the recent arrival of our small party was looked upon by most of the other inmates as a possible invasion of their privacy.

Food supplies had reached a disastrously low level: thin soup, ersatz coffee, a few potatoes and a daily portion of bread and margarine did little to foster a feeling of well-being and long before nine o'clock, tired, hungry and bored stiff, most of us would drift into a welcome sleep.

As newcomers, we were automatically selected to join the quarry party and our day, beginning at around six a.m., would see us very quickly on our way to the stone face where we were expected not only to extract the stone by means of hacking or prising it free from the face, but to roll it down to the bottom of the quarry and, after grading according to size, load it into a series of metal skips lined up in a train on a narrow gauge railway. The expected manual output was, I believe, laid down at the rate of fifteen skips per prisoner per day and although on many occasions the Germans had refused to allow us to leave until a satisfactory quota of stone had been worked, the over-ambitious target of fifteen skips was never met.

In early December, already suffering badly blistered hands brought on by this arduous task − our only tools comprised an unusable short, blunt pick, an overlarge fork with just three prongs and a cumbersome shovel − I had decided that with the weather, low rations and a rabid dislike of anything German, I must try to opt out of this uncivilised occupation.

This was perhaps easier said than done but, without thinking too deeply on the matter, I deliberately allowed a large rock to fall on my extended wrist. The result of this was that I suffered a minor fracture and was taken under escort back to the billet. The pain although, I suppose, moderately unpleasant, was over-compensated for by way of my newly-found freedom from work. A quick check by our so far blissfully redundant French Canadian medical orderly confirmed the breakage and that very same night I was taken under escort on a journey of several miles along the railway line to a much larger labour camp situated in Oppeln.

A German doctor of great age ponderously probed and twisted my wrist before finally pronouncing it broken and in need of minor repair. This was duly carried out and I was returned to our camp with a recommendation that I should be given light work only for one month. No doubt a situation such as this makes one feel for the sanity of the Germans as, realising that I could no longer wield a pick or shovel, they gave me a job pushing the loaded skips as best I could using my back as a means of propulsion rather than my hands. I suppose in a manner of speaking life in this semi-encapsulated backwater could best be described as a state where one possibly lived for a brief moment with the remainder of one's time sadly consisting of an indeterminable series of extremely demoralising patches of grey.

We witnessed the almost daily bombing raids carried out by the Yanks whose Flying Fortresses glinted bright and silver in the weak wintry sun as they courageously pushed along so very deep into enemy territory. Each aircraft, although unquestionably moving under considerable stress, unswervingly pressed ahead of a long white trail of vapour that almost, it seemed, lent itself to an air of festivity. These signs we knew were a symbol of hope. News was scarce, in fact what little news we received was of German origin and therefore could be truly discounted as being the Gospel according to Adolf. Snow was rapidly becoming a major problem and for as far as the eye could see there was nothing but a thick blanket which never seemed to go away. Manual efforts to clear the snow were scarcely enough to keep a rough path clear of the stuff. There was a serious shortage of fuel to tend the ancient combustion stove and even then a certain proportion of that had to be put aside to provide us with a once a week strip wash in hot water.

Christmas was rapidly approaching and this, even under these unhappy circumstances, was clearly responsible for creating a for once united atmosphere. Although at this stage it was no more than a rumour, the talk going around was of a whole day off work, an extra ration of soup − that is, one at mid-day and one later on in the day, which rumour persisted would be further highlighted by the issue of an individual Christmas cake per man, kindly, it was thought, to be donated by the faceless proprietor of the stone quarry.

Expectations knew no bounds and as the day approached, the feeling of excitement dramatically escalated to a new peak. Several facts had now been confirmed. Rumours previously whispered about were about to become reality and in addition to all this was the greatest treat of all. We were to be escorted on Christmas morning for a joint service to be held at a neighbouring camp where we would be allowed to spend approximately one hour with the inmates who now numbered amongst their group Jock and Ben, neither of whom I had seen since the split up on the outskirts of Waldenstein railway station.

Christmas Eve arrived. We had worked our usual stint, we'd been as cold and as hungry as ever, but somehow this day and the day to follow would be magic. Hastening back to our billet that night, we flung ourselves feverishly into an absolute orgy of cleaning. We cleaned the fresh wet snow from our sadly ageing boots and set to with a will to spruce them up with a mixture of soot, recently obtained from the combustion stove chimney, and axle grease, most likely liberated from the axle boxes of the stone wagons.

Some enterprising type came up with a rusting but otherwise usable flat iron which was in constant demand until the early hours of Christmas morning. This time, although the lights had been switched off at nine p.m., we didn't sleep. Trousers and jackets were pressed by the light of several temporary lamps made from cans filled with a foul-smelling oil and supporting a floating wick of slow burning string.

The great morning finally arrived. We stayed in bed for a little while luxuriating in our newly-found but all too temporary life of leisure. A can of weak substitute coffee was bubbling on an unusually hot stove, bread was already being divided into equal slices and soon every inmate was, contentedly, for once, sitting up in bed eating, drinking and doing exactly nothing.

Being totally unaccustomed to this life of ease, it become pressingly obvious that we must rise and prepare for our march through the main street of Waldenstein where we truly expected to make a dash with the local villagers and then carry on towards the other camp for our Christmas service. The guards, already fidgeting outside the camp gates, looked a down-at-heel bunch with their shabby ill-fitting uniforms woefully lacking even a mere shadow of their former glory. All the guards had been turned out to escort us, most probably because we would, for a short time anyway, be leaving behind us an empty camp as all on this particular occasion had decided to take advantage of the offer to join for a short while our friends in the other camp. There was of course, another factor concerning the presence of all the guards. No leave had been granted to anyone because, we imagined, the rail network was stretched to an absolute limit and no matter where the guards' families lived, this part of Germany, Silesia, was in such a God-forsaken neck of the woods as to deter even the stoutest heart from attempting to travel any great distance under such trying conditions. Long John, as the name implies, was most likely the tallest member of the Wehrmacht we had so far come up against. Woefully thick, unnecessarily loud in his speech and hailing from some distant part of Austria, he could be heard complaining in his whining gutteral voice of everything in creation and with the Engländers taking pride of place at the top of his hate list.

We set off at a good pace, very much in step, leaving our guards to slip and slide uncertainly across the frozen snow. As we had expected, the entire village, or so it seemed, had turned out to witness this happening of a lifetime and they, appraising us with a certain respect, must surely have had cause to wonder which of us were the captives and which were the captors.

A necessary slackening of our pace was, however, prompted by the inability of the guards who, finding it difficult to keep abreast of us, were beginning to feel slightly inferior and had begun to resort to a number of loudly-voiced threats which could after all have seriously curtailed our visit to the camp had we not quite wisely taken the hint and reduced our speed to a more acceptable pace. Our arrival at the camp was her-alded by a warm sense of comradeship and the short service, very well organised, was soon under way. The preparations for what took place must have taken an enormous amount of time. Handwritten hymn sheets had been painstakingly produced with a number of the more popular Christmas carols including of course everyone's favourite, 'Silent Night', and these were sung with respectful enthusiasm. Prayers were said and a prepared lesson was read and a short sermon given by one of the prisoners, and with a final gesture of feeling and defiance we gave an enthusiastic rendition of our National Anthem. The service thus ending allowed a little time for us to circulate and offer our wishes to our opposite numbers in the camp. Jock and Ben were as pleased to see me as I was to see them. Naturally at this time of the year in ordinary circumstances one would be offered refreshment and a toast of some description but such niceties were casually brushed aside without any thought of embarrassment.

Our return journey, carried out in a style similar to our outward march, was uneventful, although without doubt we had scored a hit with the locals and, I suspect, we had possibly gained some reluctant respect from our captors.

Back in our own familiar quarters, things never quite reached the climax we had anticipated — far too many thoughts of those at home in England were now creeping in to dominate our day. The promised individual Christmas cakes had turned up disappointingly in the shape and texture of an ordinary iced bun. The rest of the day simply dragged by and long before the appointed hour for 'lights out' we were already seeking the comfort and isolation of our own thoughts before finally dropping off into a thankful sleep which closed the last chapter on this day of peace and goodwill to all men.

Christmas seemed rapidly to fade from our immediate thoughts. There was a change of mood difficult to pinpoint but nevertheless tinged with a feeling of expectancy. The air-raids, no doubt curtailed by the bad weather, had ceased to become a daily feature of our lives. The sound of gunfire seldom seemed to abate and in fact had gradually but persistently increased both in volume and intensity. Could it possibly happen, we wondered, that the Russians would finally over-run the area, would they perhaps by-pass us, or, worse still, would the Germans attempt to move us deeper into Germany?

CHAPTER EIGHT

Waldenstein (Arbeitskommando) Silesia
A walk in the wild

Little did we realise that this particular morning was to be the most significant event we had so far experienced. Dates never counted for very much but, having been awakened at an unearthly hour − difficult to actually pinpoint but certainly long before dawn − I distinctly remember my first conscious thoughts were to dwell on the bellicose cries of the guards frenetically milling around in the deep snow outside our hut. We began to realise that, for good or evil, this day was to be the start of something different − it was.

We were herded out into the grim, snow covered compound with the few worldly goods we possessed. Sporadic shelling could be distinctly heard and, with the stillness of the frozen air, the sounds seemed to be scarcely more than a few miles distant. The Ruskies, bless 'em, were certainly livening things up. Before moving off, we were joined by the chaps from the nearby labour camp whom we had been able to visit for an all too brief time on Christmas Day, so again, at least for the present, I was able to link up with Jock and Ben.

Speculation was quite naturally rife − what did the Jerry intend to do with us? Why were we set to walk in the direction of the gunfire instead of away from it and, when, most important of all, were we likely to get a bite of something to eat and a drink?

Before we had been very long on our way we were to witness for the first time a pathetically new form of childish punishment. It became clear that the head count repeated several times before leaving the camp had somehow been incorrect. One of our inmates had managed unbeknown to the guards to take off in the hope that perhaps he could make his way through to the Russian lines, but unfortunately he had decided to chance it along the railway tracks and had been picked up within a very short time by a German patrol standing guard at a nearby railway bridge.

Upon his return to the fold, the column was halted and the offender, having first been made to remove the braces and belt from his trousers, was ordered to pull a very heavily laden sledge belonging to the guards with one hand whilst holding up his trousers with the other. Credit to him, he did just that for the rest of the day in a temperature way below freezing and without the benefit of even a pair of gloves to give protection against the bitterly cold wind. By mid-morning we had arrived at the industrial town of Oppeln and here we were ushered into an old derelict factory that had until now served as a very large labour camp and where I had wasted my time on a recent visit to see the doctor. The situation was chaotic, we were directed to the far end of this bleak workhouse-like shell of a building. The strength of our party had, I should imagine, been somewhere in the region of 40 men but our ranks had now been swelled by several other small groups culled from I know not where plus of course the rather large group who had been using the building as living and sleeping quarters.

All in all, I should imagine that the entire party which, although unbeknown to us at that time, was to stay with us for many months to come, added to our party, now made a full total of perhaps 300 men.

As I already mentioned in the previous chapter, food throughout this bitter winter had, to say the least, been pathetically inadequate so it can well be imagined how we responded to the news that here before our very eyes was an absolute mountain of Red Cross food parcels far, far more in fact than we had ever dreamed of and, we were warned, all stocks that couldn't be carried away were to be left behind as waste.

We had half an hour during which time we managed to consume as much food as possible. This didn't present any problem at all but we were all deeply angry to realise that, hungry as we had been, here was a supply of food freely donated, in the main, by the Canadian Red Cross, transported across the Atlantic all at a very great risk to our Merchant Seamen, then given to hungry chaps who just couldn't eat it all and all of us knowing that the remaining enormous

stockpile of precious food would fall into the hands of either
the Germans or the Russians. I don't know who was responsible, was it perhaps German bureaucracy? Was it over-prudent
rationing by bungling Allied camp officials? Or, in an attempt
to be charitable, had it arrived via the Protecting Powers sadly
too short a time before this mass evacuation took place?

Whatever the reason was, we gluttonously stuffed our
shrunken stomachs with this rich food. Powdered milk mixed
with water, raisins, butter and jam did wonders to satiate our
long-term hunger. For most of us however, there was the
inevitable price to pay for such an excess as we were soon
to succumb to the most painful stomach pains followed by
violent bouts of sickness and diarrhoea. Bodies lay everywhere
and amidst all the stench and suffering, we were ordered to
move on.

Our journey that day was truly a day to forget, we crossed
the Oder in a blinding snowstorm unable to see but a few
yards ahead. Walking across the frozen wastes of Silesia in
the harsh unrelenting grip of winter is enough for any human
being. To be caught out, inadequately clothed, in the midst
of a raging blizzard with a temperature down to God knows
what depth would have been sufficient, but to trudge along
doggedly plodding our way with a cumbersome supply of Red
Cross parcels strung uncomfortably across our shoulders with
strips of rag or string and wading through the deep snow
with additional parcels clutched one under each arm made
this exercise a true feat of endurance.

Oh dear, oh dear, how we smelt. Unable to stop for the
many frequent and insistent calls of nature, our trousers had
now become our personal ccsspits. The cold was so severe
with the strong wind gusting the snow and ice on our faces,
that our breath began to freeze around the mouth. This
caused small icicles to form and a hoar-like frost stretched the
flesh around the lower jaw, the nose and the mouth, making
it all far too much of an effort to speak.

We had literally staggered along our way oblivious of time
or direction and on account of our late start out from Oppeln
coupled with the fact that it was mid-winter, darkness began
to fall long before there was any sign of a let-up in our
progress to nowhere. A German scout party had gone on
ahead of the column seeking a suitable place to put us
up for the night but, returning after a fruitless search we

were, of necessity, forced to continue walking until long after darkness. The noise of the advancing Russian guns and the retreating German artillery could be heard encouragingly close and with the overcast sky spasmodically illuminated by the flash of the guns and the ever-dazzling whiteness of the snow, we pressed on until finally coming across a large dutch style barn housing a fair sprinkling of straw. Most of us carried a small can of some description adequate enough to heat up sufficient water to make a brew. Somehow, after completing a scavenging expedition round the barn, we managed to come up with enough bits and pieces of wood to start a small fire and, managing to scrounge a light from one of the many fires already burning, we set to with a will to first melt the ice and snow, and after a painstakingly long wait we finally succeeded in producing a hot drink.

After the exertions of the day and following the earlier over-indulgence of food, we were more than content just to huddle together covering ourselves as best we could with the somewhat scant amount of straw at our disposal.

One ill-considered move we made was to cause problems the following morning when, shortly after daybreak we were roused by our guards and told to be ready to move off in 30 minutes time. The previous night, before dropping off into a spasmodic sleep, we had removed our boots, and what a mistake that was! Picking up each boot in turn, we were all to discover that they had frozen rock hard and, try as we might, we just couldn't get into them again.

The obvious solution would of course have been to light a fire and gradually thaw them out but with the short period of time available to us, this was just not possible. The only solution immediately available was to urinate on them and as the warmth of the urine temporarily softened the leather, there was a mad scramble to get them on again before the fluid turned into ice.

Outside the blizzard continued to rage as indeed it continued to howl and blow for many days following. Our march continued with a bleak monotonous regularity. We walked all day, talked little and chose to keep our thoughts very much to ourselves. Each day before dusk we were usually lucky enough to come across a farm of some description containing barns or outbuildings likely to provide enough space to house us for the night.

Thanks to our food parcels we had an abundant level of the vitamins we required but carrying this extra weight and trudging through the deep, strength-sapping snow, gave us cause for concern. A feeling of isolation, of unrelenting cold, and our consistently grinding, churning stomachs made us look like a very miserable column of refugees? hostages? P.O.W.s? We just didn't know.

What we did know was that the penetrating bitter cold was numbing our minds as well as our bodies. The area we were moving through appeared to be completely evacuated. We seldom saw a living soul, either human or animal. There was, of course, the ever-prevalent sound of gunfire but, due to the persistently bad weather, all aerial action was at that moment completely off the menu. We walked and walked in a kind of limbo. We didn't speak, the guards didn't speak, it was I suppose like living in some form of suspended animation. We remembered things past, we had no understandable present and we approached the future with a mixture of hope and trepidation.

Since leaving Oppeln we had come across several road signs although the places mentioned meant little or nothing to us. My only observation was that unlike our own country where, fearing a German invasion all road signs had been removed, here the Germans either didn't think that way or else they had been grossly over-confident, never pausing even for a second to consider the possibility of an invading force running wild over the Fatherland. I can only remember one particular sign that pointed to a place called Neustadt.

We were covering, or so we thought, about 20 miles a day. Not seeing the sun, it was difficult to estimate in which direction we were heading. The noise of shell fire continued uninterrupted on our left, neither seeming to increase or diminish, which proved that we were, if the Russians were advancing from the East, travelling in a westerly direction.

Without calendars or watches and with each day being an uneasy energy-sapping repetition of the previous one, it was difficult to even recognise any particular day as being different from another. As the weeks passed by, a change in the weather became noticeable. The snow continued to fall but not by any means with the blizzard-like intensity of the early days. The countryside still lay under a thick blanket of snow. Civilian refugees, shabbily clad, were seen pulling a few miserable belongings on an odd assortment of sledges, most of which appeared to be crudely hand made. The sky, now more frequently clear of cloud, brought out the German Stuka dive-bombers nervously and hesitantly making their way east in the direction of the front line in the all-too-forlorn hope of stemming the tide of an army now hell bent on making a final push towards Berlin. The distance beween the Russians and ourselves could, at this point, have been no greater than 8–10 miles and the noise of battle had reached an almost deafening roar. Strange as it was, although the Russians undoubtedly had the upper hand, at no time did we see a single Russian aircraft. From this, it was thought that Ivan was concentrating his mass superiority on land forces and simply bulldozing his way through from Poland. Sadly, our food stocks had dwindled to absolutely nothing. Inadequately clothed against the sub-zero temperatures, we were now beginning to lose several of the chaps who had gone down with either frostbite, exhaustion or dysentery. A horse-drawn cart had materialised virtually from nowhere and the sick were loaded and taken away on this vehicle.

Due to either sheer apathy or a general numbness of our minds we never once sought to enquire as to the fate of these people.

Survival became an obsession: we would quarrel and bicker over even a morsel of raw sugar beet. The guards, who had so far been relieved of the task of feeding us due to our self-sufficiency in food, were now faced daily with the task of not only guarding us, moving us and finding shelter for each nights' halt, but also with feeding us.

Our very irregular diet consisted, in the main, of an occasional biscuit-type crispbread very similar to Ryvita and called Knäckebrot, a much less frequent ration of two or three potatoes per man or perhaps a sugar beet, the latter being liberated by ourselves from the odd farms as we passed by.

Drinks required a great deal of inventiveness. We did from time to time manage a small quantity of 'tea' – made from dried hawthorn leaves – or a small amount of 'coffee' produced from acorns. With the limited degree of scope available, we would somehow manage to get a brew of 'tea' or 'coffee' going over a small fire, which would also serve to bake the potatoes although in the case of the sugar beet, indigestable as it was, chewing it in its raw state simply

made it last longer. The flavour of sugar beet, Heaven forbid
that one would be so unwise as to taste it, was so disgusting
that it just wasn't worth the effort of attempting to disguise
it by cooking. I mustn't make the mistake of making this a
hard-luck story, it certainly isn't intended that way, and to
qualify this point, it must be emphasised that, apart from an
altogether infrequent issue of the odd small can of processed
meat, our captors fared little better than we. Their clothing,
in the main, was secondhand, shabby and, in most cases,
ill-fitting, and was, if anything, less likely to give protection
against the cold than ours. Where they did score was with
their caps, which had pull-down ear flaps, and they also
had gloves. For footwear they had what seemed to be fairly
strong, if sometimes ill-fitting, boots and, like ourselves,
instead of socks, they wore triangular pieces of cloth which,
on account of their ability to slip and slide inside the boot,
were very uncomfortable. I believe these were called 'Fuss
schläfers' – 'Foot sleepers'.

In addition to these problems we also had cause for concern
in respect of personal hygiene. For several weeks past we
had been unable to wash or shave in any way other than
in purely primitive conditions which, coupled with our now
meagre diet, simply brought along in its wake positive hordes
of body lice which were to be our unwelcome guests during
the weeks that followed.

True, however, to the characteristic trait of the British,
renowned for their ability to overcome adversity, we subconsciously had come to terms with our situation and the general
attitude had done a remarkable turn about from stunned
apathy to heightening optimism. We began to communicate
with each other again. Even the guards had once more become
the butt of our subtle sarcasm which, although it made us feel
better, somehow seemed to create a more aggressive attitude
towards us.

I had, since the first day out, resumed my friendship with
'Jock'. We had been in the same barrack hut at Klimontow
and having been transferred together to Waldenstein, had
had the misfortune to be split between the two labour camps
so it had been a great morale booster to meet up once more.
As I've already said, for the first part of our journey we were
too involved with our personal survival to say very much but
his being there had still felt good and supportive.

'Jock' had been a prisoner since his capture at St. Valery at the time of Dunkirk. He had served with the 51st Highland Division and in civilian life worked as a coal miner. Unfortunately, as surnames had meant so little to us, each one had very quickly become known either by one's Christian name or by a nickname. He was short, thick set, with black hair and was a loyal and decent friend.

One might think that being a coal miner certainly contrasts with a scholarly aptitude to converse very capably in German. However, Jock did speak good German and, more important still, he had the unfailing ability to understand and profit from a natural talent which allowed him to slip quite easily into conversation with a guard and, having found his weakness, set about reducing him to a whimpering manic-depressive quicker than the average German could say 'Heil Hitler'!

At this particular time, Jock's target was a small, woefully insignificant member of the Master Race with the look of a half-wit and an oversized uniform to match. Jock had already found out that this chap was married and that his wife and two daughters lived in Silesia, an area which we knew was even then being rapidly over-run by Ivan. We also noted with some satisfaction that his daily ration of food was habitually secreted in the right-hand pocket of his huge flapping greatcoat.

Our plan of action was quite simple. Jock would approach him from the left-hand side and depressingly relate to 'Dopey', as this guard was known, a horrific story spiced with graphic detail of Ivan's partiality towards German women and in particular to 'Dopey's' women. Having begun the process of winding up his victim, Jock would further expound on the insatiable sexual appetite of the Ruskies. At this stage, with Jock having successfully wound up 'Dopey' to the point of self-destruction, I would gently slip my hand into his right-hand pocket, extract his food ration and fall further back in the column to avoid any possibility of detection. Now, with discipline being extremely strict in the German Army, 'Dopey' would prefer to silently lament the sudden, irrevocable liberation of his rations rather than risk punishment by admitting his loss. For obvious reasons, this stunt couldn't be exploited too often as one can well imagine the consequence of being caught out. On one occasion, just to quote an example of the perfidious nature of the Hun, we were halted for a short break just beside the front garden of a small farmhouse. One member of our party, scavenging around a rather unhealthy-looking compost heap, espied a few rotting onions sticking out of the top. With his whoop of delight attracting several of us to his 'find', we all gleefully began hauling out this feast of decaying onions. Although Jock and I and a few others managed to secrete our ill-gotten gains, many other were caught out by Jerry and made to return the onions to the compost heap.

Rumours were again beginning to circulate. The weather had recently shown a remarkable improvement, which in turn had brought out literally thousands and thousands of refugees and the frantic efforts of the Nazis to squash any signs of panic amongst the now teeming hordes was at times like this proving a much too difficult situation to handle.

People were being turned back along the road from whence they had come both by civilian and military police. Small children frantically searching for lost parents, old folk, cold, hungry and bewildered, all had come together with absolutely nowhere to go. In the out-lying fields we could see young boys in their very early teens being taught the rudimentary skills of bearing arms using brush handles and other pieces of wood as imitation weapons.

The Stukas continued their fruitless attempt to slow down the Russian advance. Old men had been brought from their rocking chairs to nervously don the government issue armband which identified them as reluctant, but full-blooded members of the Volkstürm, a body similar to our own Home Guard. Most distressing of all was the all-too-frequent sight of inmates conscripted from some local concentration camp, ill-clad in their striped pyjama-like clothing and wearing the yellow star of David on their back. Shuffling around in an assortment of ill-fitting canvas shoes with wooden soles and with the wind and freezing hail cutting through their thin clothing, they were being forced by the black-uniformed S.S. guards to erect road blocks along strategic sections of the road.

We were later to become accustomed to this alarming sight but could never accept the brutal action of the S.S. who considered it necessary to shoot and kill one prisoner in cold blood at each work site simply to exhort the remaining unfortunates to a greater effort. The tragedy of this criminal act was blatantly apparent on every road block we passed by. Compulsively gazing in horror at these sadly abused people made all the previous rumours we had heard about their treatment only too regrettably understood. I never saw the inside of any of the notorious concentration camps but, having seen the condition of these unfortunates who must have been considered 'fitter' than the ones left in the camps, then one needs only to speculate as to the appalling condition of the remainder.

More hastily-arranged night shelters designed, I suppose, to give us minimum comfort with the emphasis on maximum security from the German point of view. More refugees, to congest the already crowded roads, more reluctant Hitler Youths indoctrinated and coerced into even more reluctant fighting men as they swung across the open fields unhappily flourishing their wooden make-believe guns in response to the constant exhortations of their despairing instructors.

Food had again become a problem. I suppose that under these conditions of stress and shortage it would prove a Herculean task to find sufficient means of support for a small group but for our party, possibly 300 strong, it was an ever-increasing problem. For the uninitiated, I would hasten to dissuade all from that culinary delight, Sugar Beet Soup! Even to hungry men, the only satisfying feature was its warmth.

It was perhaps around mid-February that we came across a large prison camp. The layout, we noted, was pretty identical to the general run of these establishments apart from the fact that the barrack-like huts here were raised two or three feet above ground level which, under the circumstances, was just as well because this camp was absolutely bursting at the seams with inmates of all nationalities and we were bedded down for the night underneath these huts.

Up to an early start, we were again off on our journey to nowhere. The events of the previous night gave some food for thought as, although the camp was a teeming mass of humanity, none of us appeared to have conversed with anyone other than our immediate travelling companions, although I remember someone did say that it was known as Stalag Luft III, and that, you most probably know, was the notorious camp from which the 'Great Escape' had taken place. Many

R.A.F. Officers had participated in the mass escape but sadly, on being recaptured, most of them had been brutally murdered by the S.S. A few days' march from here saw a sudden, be it but brief change from normal routine. Passing through a small village, we came across a very bloated and very dead cow lying by the side of the road. This animal had obviously expired some days previously, hence the grossly inflated stomach distended by the creation of gases from within the decomposing corpse. The Germans, like ourselves, were terribly hungry and, unable to resist the temptation, they brought us to a halt and asked for a volunteer with experience of butchering. Fortunately for us, we did in fact have a chap who, rightly or wrongly, professed to be of that ilk. He was given a jackknife and a bayonet and set to with a will, to carve up this stinking carcass. Very little further movement along the road followed our find. Small fires sprung up from nowhere, meat could be seen and smelt cooking in cans and in some cases being roasted to a cinder on open wood fires. A potato clamp had been spotted in a nearby farm and was being enthusiastically looted for its contents. What a feast we had. Baked potatoes and putrefied lumps of cow meat washed down with a milk and sugar-less cup of acorn coffee was a feast fit for the Gods. Goodness knows to what we owed our immunity from food poison. Septic sores, beri-beri, blisters and frost bite, we all had our share, but no matter what we managed to scavenge and eat, outbreaks of food poisoning were thankfully, extremely rare.

Three months or more had passed since leaving Waldenstein and during that time we had not been able to get a decent wash. Clothing was beginning to smell, footwear was wearing out and body lice were becoming an increasing irritation. One particular source of satisfaction was that of seeking to preserve our teeth. Perhaps under any given circumstance, one tends to become obsessional about relatively small matters. Freud probably had an answer to it but suffice to say an inexplicable fixation on the welfare of our teeth served to provide a minor diversion from ordinary affairs. This obsession was to reach a peak when, having bedded down one night in a group of abandoned stables, we had found a rather large cache of rock salt which had been supplied for the use of the horses because, correctly or otherwise, it was considered that by licking this salt, a horse would remain immune to colic.

Someone, chipping off a piece of this salt, suggested that covering one's finger with a small piece of dampened rag coated with a small quantity of rock salt and applying it to the teeth and gums would act as a protection against decay. I must say it certainly did no harm but whether it did any good was another matter.

The weather had improved, the snow storms had abated. Snow still covered the ground and showed a marked reluctance to disappear. It must have been early March, and according to the old lags, we could soon expect the slightly less chilling welcome of an early spring. The dire shortage of food had brought about an increased feeling of weakness coupled with other debilitating factors such as minor frost bite mainly on our hands and feet and our daily mileage rate had fallen to around six or seven miles per day. It was pretty obvious that we just couldn't continue with things being what they were and indeed, with the rate of sickness increasing daily, we were brought to a halt at a rather large farm on the outskirts of a village named Drauskowitz which lay approximately seven miles from the industrial town of Bautzen.

It seemed that no one knew exactly what was happening. We had a so-called 'Man of Confidence' whose job it was to liaise with the Jerry on matters concerning our welfare. He was a sergeant who, had he been of a stronger nature, would, I feel sure, have solved many of our sometimes unnecessary problems. We suggested to him that he find out exactly why we were where we were and what, if anything, could be done to alleviate our present predicament.

As usual, his efforts were completely negative. We were given to understand that, pending further instructions from some faceless warlord in the Wehrmacht, we were to remain, at any rate for the time being, confined within this rather securely walled-in farm.

CHAPTER NINE
Drauskowitz – Saxony. The farm.
Death of a friend

Our stay here was to last for about four weeks and I suppose in a way we were more than pleased to get off the dreary never-ending roads. We were all billeted in the one barn which fortunately held a good supply of straw to bed down on. The building had no windows and entrance and exit was through the one double door which opened onto the enclosed courtyard. It had long been a recognised habit to merge into small groups which were widely known as syndicates. Perhaps this could be due to a primitive tribal instinct by which means we somehow hoped to provide each other with a sense of warmth and protection. Another reason for the formation of these syndicates was that we were able to choose people of a similar temperament to our own as, living so closely together, a clash of personalities could become disastrous and when it was necessary, as indeed it frequently was, to pool one's rations for the purpose of cooking or for strict economy then a group syndicate became the obvious answer.

Our syndicate comprised five prisoners (myself included). We had Jock, my little Scottish mining friend and late of the 51st Highland Division, we had Jeff – don't know much about him but he did something in Nottingham in civilian life – and his friend Ron who owned a small grocer's shop somewhere in Hull. Our star member, by universal acceptance, was 'Ben'. Everyone of us has, at some stage in our lives, known a 'Ben', he's usually a likeable character but possessed with the unfortunate aptitude of an old time slap-stick comedian predictably renowned for getting things wrong. He's not a forager, he's not even a thinker but, as if to compensate for all his shortcomings, there is always the disarming smile of an innocent – that's how it was with Ben.

Take as an example our obsessive urge to survive often with the help of a little illicitly-gained food. Ben just hadn't got the ability to scrounge. If we liberated a few potatoes or a handful of barley, Ben couldn't be relied upon even to the extent of boiling up a few spuds. He'd accidentally put out the fire, burn himself or the food – in fact in a cultural wasteland such as this, he was a natural disaster. Yet for all these shortcomings there was the one memorable day when Ben was to temporarily rise above all expectations. In an isolated corner of the farm dominated by a substantial and exceptionally high wall was the communal latrine. Now with most people suffering from some peculiar form of stomach trouble, this was never regarded as a particularly favourite corner on which to linger, so, on account of this, the guards patrolling the outer wall made a practice of giving this corner a pretty wide berth. Sympathetic forced labourers working in the fields surrounding the farm were aware of this and, by custom and practice, would, whenever possible, surreptitiously toss a few sugar beet over the wall. This corner was usually thronged with prisoners hopefully awaiting the anticipated arrival of this manna from Heaven, ever mindful of the fact that even the more sturdy types could be felled in the twinkling of an eye during the mad scramble that took place once the beet started to fly over the wall.

It happened that out of sheer frustration and in a last-gasp attempt to get Ben away from under our feet, we sent him out in search of sugar beet. It must be expressly understood that we in no way expected a result, we simply wanted him to activate himself somewhere beyond recall, and so our surprise could be well imagined when, in the short space of possibly five or six minutes, Ben was to return with the most enormous sugar beet the world had ever witnessed.

Back slapping and congratulations quickly became the order of the day, a sharpened piece of metal was hastily produced and then, having cut up the beet, we ate it so very quickly under the benign and shyly satisfied gaze of Ben – the founder of the feast. 'How did you manage to beat the scrum and get this delectable fat sugar beet?' we asked. With a sly grin Ben said that he'd rather not say but we eventually managed to get the truth out of him. It appears that it flew over the wall and disappeared into the slimy depths of the well-patronised cess pit. Ben, however, assured us in his usual disarming matter-of-fact fashion that there was never a need to worry – he'd washed the thing in cold water and wiped it in straw before we had eaten it! The camp kitchen's huge boilers, commissioned in more peaceful times to boiling up cattle fodder, were now producing drastically-reduced supplies of potato soup or alternatively that infamous German concoction, acorn coffee. Little wonder that our subsidised and irregular ration of sugar beet was needed to supplement an otherwise thin diet.

Boredom had reached new heights. The rest, if not the food, had worked wonders and the dubious luxury of a cold water tap situated outside the kitchen proved a novel addition to our scant amenities although, with the weather being what it was, none but the most hardy beings amongst us were to take advantage of this one offer we were able to refuse. We hadn't yet got used to the shock of washing – let alone under the freezing cold water that gushed out of the tap.

Rumour had it that we were to have a hot shower and sure enough, and in the fullness of time, we were escorted in organised groups along the road to Bautzen. This trek covered 6 or 7 miles each way and I would sincerely say that Bautzen was the least lovable town in the whole of Germany. Our approach towards the centre was via a partly derelict industrial area which had either been bombed almost flat or else the factories had fallen into an awfully sad state of repair. Perhaps the same thing could also be said about the depressing commercial centre. The people on the streets looked drab, grey and apprehensive, in fact very far removed, we thought, from their former arrogance. A few antiquated trams clanked and ground their unending way to wherever trams are wont to go. The military were there in force although there was little sign of what I would call 'war-like troops'. Most of the Jerries seemed to be either elderly base troops, badly disabled soldiers and, of course, the pathetic, very elderly and shabbily turned out Volkstürm (Home Guard). Bolstering up morale, or rather desperately trying to, huge swastika flags – symbols of a dying cause – fluttered limply from both offices and public buildings alike. Our immediate goal, the public baths, was quickly reached, in at one end, clothes off for fumigation, a very quick shower followed by an exhaustive delousing session after which we were rudely propelled back into the changing-room looking more like ill-nourished ghosts than satisfied customers. Our clothes, dumped in a heap, were unmarked and time was evidently short judging by the persistent baying of the guards screeching their eternal 'Raus' and whose paramount obsession in life was to get back before dusk, so it was a case of grabbing what looked like fitting and take a chance. On our way back, I chanced to join up with Jack Pedersen, a New Zealander who I believe had been taken prisoner during the African campaign of 1941. He had been in the same hut as me at Waldenstein and although so far we hadn't actually conversed a lot, I found him to be a quite likeable character. We chatted as we walked and he told me about his farm in Raurimu, New Zealand and about his wife and home life. We could still hear the Russian guns rumbling away in the distance and the conversation gradually changed to our having a joint desire to take off from this farm and hopefully get through to the Russian lines. Little more was said although we did agree to talk again sometime during the following day. Talk we eventually did, and in the cold light of the day, much of our original enthusiasm for breaking out seemed to have evaporated. The way things appeared to be going gave every indication that, travelling at the limited speed which we had been moving at, the Russians might soon break through and hopefully release us. Perhaps we could be excused this bout of indecision but when one thinks hard enough, one realises the mental pressures and general state of confusion which we all suffered from. We had had no news whatsoever for many months past, we assumed the invasion was going well but we still had no idea what was happening other than that the Russians were on the doorstep.

We also wondered where we were going, how far and why? Would there be food at the end of it all or were we, as some thought, being herded to a central point possibly in Bavaria or somewhere similar where we could be used as hostages or even, as the most doubting pessimists would have it, were we being taken somewhere to be disposed of? It was all very disturbing. A few prisoners had tried their hand at escaping and without exception had been 'shot whilst trying to escape' and their bodies sometimes returned to the column. Food was of such poor quality and quantity as to be of little use as a means of sustenance, our clothing was almost threadbare and our boot soles almost non-existent. We had used paper or cardboard to line the area where the soles had once been although now, due to a shortage of these commodities, we were packing in straw.

General deficiencies on all fronts had brought on a new spate of dysentery and beri-beri. The weakening effort of either one would have been sufficient enough to warrant, under normal conditions, hospitalization but here even a warm bed was out of the question. Beri-beri was the most debilitating of the two and at this time was thought to be rheumatism of the joints which caused a swelling. It was only later on that we were to discover more information about it.

Small cuts had begun to fester, minor attacks of frostbite would cause others to hobble about and the most vexatious feature was that our so-called sanitäter, the French Canadian medical orderly from Waldenstein had temporarily mislaid his stock of paper bandages and whatever else he had. Therefore, our only means of keeping infection down was to make use of the liberal supply of cold water which, after all, was better than nothing.

This has perhaps been digressing from the original point but in deciding whether or not to 'go for gold' and try to reach the Russians one had to deliberate to the full.

The reasons against were mainly that at this stage of the war, escaping prisoners once recaptured weren't being greeted with open arms. Were we fit enough? And above all was it so close to the end that it was perhaps better to sit and wait. Jack's main reason against escaping was that he was married and had been a prisoner for a long while and at this late stage rightly felt the risk to be too great.

Reluctant as he was, I did finally manage to overcome his reservations and we decided that, as this particular day was pretty foul with lots of sleet and cloud, the night would more likely be very much the same with plenty of cover to skirt around the mud and melting snow of the parade ground.

Having since read books highlighting the expertise and the meticulous planning on offer within the more, for want of a better word, established prison camps, I can only describe our effort as being almost totally irresponsible. We first intended to carry out a midnight foray on the living quarters of a fat old hare that we had observed spending its days alternately resting and eating in a large unpadlocked hutch situated in the far corner of the compound adjoining the guard room.

This, in itself, seemed pretty stupid but caution had to be thrown to the wind. We needed a supply of food and with his natural bushman's ability, Jack didn't forsee any difficulty whatsoever in quietly approaching and breaking the neck of our unsuspecting food supply. This should, and indeed did, prove to be an easy task. The night was bitterly cold and snow was again beginning to fall. All off-duty guards were safely huddled in their quarters and on account of the high brick wall surrounding the farm, it was considered that a total of four guards at a time, each patrolling one wall, gave sufficient coverage. We had set off from the barn with a few handshakes and well-wishes. One enterprising body had fished out two cigarettes and gave us one each on the understanding that if we got the hare but didn't manage to get over the wall then he stood for a share of the booty. Having given our agreement, Jack was keen to be off but I insisted on first smoking my cigarette as for many weeks past we had not even seen any tobacco.

I felt sure that everything would go as we hoped but intuition had prompted me to think that, being cautiously pessimistic, if I smoked my cigarette but failed to either grab the hare or get out, then the cigarette, advanced by our speculative friend, would become forfeit. On the other hand, Jack chose to take this risk, reasoning that when we had put a fair distance between ourselves and the farm, then and only then would he enjoy his cigarette. We silently skirted our way around the inside perimeter, past the dimly lit windows of the guards' quarters whilst thanking our lucky stars that, because of the weather, all the off-duty guards were safely huddled inside, and quickly made our final approach towards the unsuspecting animal and within a matter of seconds, Jack was proudly holding up the dead hare for me to see. It was a huge animal, in fact it was almost the size of an over-fed terrier. The ease by which this first stage was accomplished increased our confidence as we approached the corner where the latrine tench was situated.

Now we knew the guards tended to give this corner a wide berth on account of the unpleasant smells always present and, with a recent upsurge of dysentery, even the area surrounding the pit had become a slimy quagmire of faeces. Cautiously we

slipped and slid our way to the rear of the latrine trench where
we had previously noted a mound of earth taken out when the
trench was dug, and standing at a height of possibly two feet
meant that we were able to stand on the top of it and with
arms extended, gently ease ourselves onto the top of the wall.
Jack was the first to go whilst I held on to the hare, and,
having successfully landed over the other side, he whispered
for me to gently toss the hare over to him.

It now seemed hours since we had left the barn although in
retrospect I doubt that it had been barely five minutes. We
were now both over the wall standing on a sloping stretch of
ground that, unknown to us beforehand, was only a matter
of two or three feet from the top of the wall. The snow had
deadened all sound apart from the continuous dull rumbling
of the distant Russian artillery and with a surge of adrenaline
pulsating through our bodies, we cautiously approached the
outer corner of the barn.

What happened next took place so quickly as to seem
an eternity and yet − if this can be understood − was an
encounter that was over and done with in an uncontrollable
flash. To our profound shock, there stood a guard facing us
with rifle pointed menacingly in our direction. I'm sure that
we both heard him click the bolt of the rifle home which
warned us that now, without any challenge or warning, he
was about to shoot and we both realised that our only
chance of salvation was to turn, double back up the slope
and hopefully take a flying dive over the wall. The whole area
was in pitch darkness although with the whiteness of the snow
lending itself as a perfect backdrop, we all three stood out
starkly exposed for that brief moment in time. Jack, realising
perhaps that our only chance lay in a surprise action, suddenly
yelled 'Run'. Together we ran, certainly no more than five of
six yards up the sloping ground where we both paused before
taking a dive over the wall. I heard one shot and, landing
deep in the middle of the open latrine trench on the other
side, I heard a series of feeble moans and instinctively knew
that Jack had been hit. Immediately this shot was fired, a
state of emergency swung into action, the entire guard was
turned out and started haphazardly firing several bursts in
the direction of the corner where I had landed. Mercifully,
although at that time I didn't appreciate it, I was safely
out of range of the volley of shots that were being fired

all around me simply because I was standing waist deep in excrement and with the top of the trench at least six inches above my head.

The volume of noise increased as the guards approached my position, loosing off further bursts of indiscriminate fire and all the time yelling excitedly at each other. They cautiously approached the corner where I had now become trapped. Several of them stood looking down on me and, strange as it may seem, I quite distinctly remember having a most peculiar thought: 'Is the position in which I am now standing similar to that in which a real corpse, not quite dead, might find itself looking up at a group of totally detached mourners?' I asked myself but here, getting back to basics, there were no mourners detached or otherwise, but just a bunch of unsavoury-looking guards grieving at being disturbed on a night such as it was. One guard, I recognised him as one we had frequently seen whilst on the march, looked down at me and with a huge grin told me that my 'Kamerad was Kaput', so, if I was to believe him, Jack was dead.

In shock, and frozen stiff, I placed my hands one on each side of the top of the trench and strained to lever myself out of this stinking mire when suddenly I felt a sharp pain in the back of my left hand and realised that one of the guards present had stuck me with either a knife or a bayonet. Unable to struggle any further, I slipped back into the trench and from that moment onwards everything thankfully developed into a limbo-like state of inertia.

In this unreal situation I somehow seem to remember that the wound in the back of my hand was beginning to ooze blood. I was absolutely filthy, exhausted and terribly confused. Dim recollections of the Kommandant arriving, a pole held by two Germans and a shouted order for me to grasp the pole whilst they hoisted me out are, I believe, quite specific. I also remember being taken into the guards' quarters where I had to side-step over the uncovered body of Jack who had been brought in from outside. I do remember most vividly looking down on his body which lay side by side with the pathetic body of the hare which he had so recently killed. A numbing of the mind is probably nature's way of eliminating unpleasant facts as, with a childlike thought, my immediate concern was to feel sorry that Jack hadn't been able to smoke his cigarette. Subconsciously, I was desperately trying to opt out of a very unhappy episode unaware that what had just happened would remain with me for the rest of my life.

My identity disc, worn at all times with my prison identity number, was crudely snatched from my neck before I was briskly marched back to the barn.

With the driving sleet which seemed to cut like so many sharp knives right through my wet and stinking clothing, I eventually made my way inside the barn and in a numbed state sat down just within the door. Several of the inmates were now wide awake and, I should imagine, having been disturbed by the shooting, would be talking about it and wondering exactly what had happened.

In my present condition it seemed to my way of thinking, that to rejoin my syndicate in the straw might well be considered a questionable and unacceptably anti-social act. I sat and pondered it all with the full blast of the wind and sleet driving in on me through the ill-fitting door. My resistance was indeed at a very low ebb, I felt mentally depleted and physically sapped of all energy with the numbing effect of the cold now beginning to act as an anaesthetic. Somewhat startled back to reality, I felt a hand on my shoulder and a distant voice asking if perhaps I intended to sit there and freeze to death. It came as quite a surprise and yet quite warming to feel that after all this, someone should care enough to ask. It was a chap I had frequently noticed on the march and although I had never actually spoken to him I believe he had served with the Royal Marines and he was now inviting me to go back and join him and his colleagues. My immediate reaction was to point out the filthy condition I was in but he would have none of it: 'As I said chum,' he spelt out, 'either stay here and freeze or join us.' I very much doubt if such charity would extend itself to such generous proportions in civilian life but here, as on so many occasions, I found the people with nothing had always more to give than those with plenty.

He helped me up and we threaded our way between the many recumbent figures dozing fitfully in their sparse beds of straw until we came to his little group. All told there were five of them and, briefly explaining the situation, my benefactor, genuinely concerned by my near-freezing body, hastened to pack two of his chums either side of me whilst he flattened himself on top of me in the hope of restoring some circulation.

I must have passed out rather suddenly only to be shaken awake by one of my Samaritans who, strangely enough, asked me if I had got a water bottle on me. My answer being in the negative, prompted my question 'Why do you ask?' His generous acceptance of things rather concerned me when he replied, 'Don't worry, you've pissed yourself and it's gone all over me. Try to get back to sleep.'

Shortly after daybreak we were all rather rudely disturbed by a noisy invasion of our barn by a strong posse of Jerries screaming for us all to be quiet (strange, I thought, when it was only they that seemed to be making the noise) and there in all his glory and in the midst of his troops stood the Kommandant, holding aloft in one hand an object I was to immediately recognise — my identification disc — and alongside him stood our redoubtable Man-of-Confidence.

The number on the disc was called out and the owner was instructed to identify himself. There being nothing to gain by holding back, I went forward and stood in front of the group. I was asked if my number was 130485 and, on replying in the affirmative, I was immediately trotted off to the guardroom.

So far that day, and bearing in mind all that had happened, I hadn't had a drink for pushing on eighteen hours and I was still no nearer to getting one now. Morale wise, I felt a marked uplift after discovering that having spent the night encased in straw and packed between bodies, my clothes, to a certain extent, were slowly beginning to dry out. The smell, I must hasten to add, was sufficient to make a skunk do a backward somersault, but surprisingly enough the vision of a steaming can of potato soup was much more uppermost in my thoughts, even more in fact than other bodily discomforts, including my throbbing hand.

Summoned into the Kommandant's office, I was unhappily disturbed to again have to step over Jack's body which was still lying where I had last seen it shortly after he was killed. No doubt with some minor consideration in mind, someone appeared to have hurriedly thrown a coarse paper-thin blanket over him.

Facing the Kommandant stood our Man-of-Confidence, myself and the grinning, self-righteous looking guard who had shot Jack. 'Were you,' asked the officer, 'the person who was involved in the attempted escape with the New Zealander?' I chose to deny everything which caused the Kommandant to show signs of frustration. To deny the fact that I was the one whom the guards had found in the latrine trench was a waste of time. My point of defence lay in the fact that they had literally no one able to substantiate the charge. I stuck to my story that I had been hurriedly called by nature to visit the latrine trench and no sooner had I arrived there, than I had heard a shot followed immediately by someone who, having thrown himself over the wall, collided with me and knocked me into the trench before disappearing into the darkness.

This story seemed to be accepted but I was soon to realise what a wily old bird this Jerry was. He gave an order to assemble all prisoners on the parade ground and this having been done ended in my being brought into the act. I was marched out and taken to the front of the parade where an ordinary kitchen table had been placed. The Kommandant had already mounted this table and I was prodded into joining him.

Facing the assembled prisoners, he held up my damaged left hand which, I must confess, was looking a trifle unhealthy and, breaking out in perfect English, began his impassioned speech to the hungry and restless mob of Kriegies. He had, or so he said, a great admiration for the English (Jerry always called the British 'English', much to the general annoyance of our Scots, Irish and Welsh counterparts) and this, for a start caused distant rumblings amongst those there gathered. The English, he went on, were the salt of the earth, men of honour and above all they were not liars.

Still holding up my left hand, he gave a sweeping wave with his left arm embracing all present and, in a lowering tone of admonishment, the cunning blighter came to the point of it all. He told how I had denied any involvement in the happening of the previous night and, being a believer in the English, he believed my story. However, he continued, the person he was seeking was present in the assembled throng and, therefore, if he wouldn't step forward and admit his guilt then the issue of Knäckebrot and soup, scheduled for early distribution, would be suspended.

This revelation caused an immediate uproar and I was left for a brief moment to consider my unenviable position. For starters, I couldn't for one second stick to my denial at the expense of three hundred or so starving prisoners. I must also hasten to add that, generous in their attitude as they were, a hungry man is likely to fall short on compassion where food is involved.

My left wrist had been released from his grip and, in a gesture of pure resignation, I simply told him that it was indeed I that he was looking for. Left standing there whilst the remainder were dismissed to the barn, I will say that several, on passing where I stood, were supportive enough to call out that I shouldn't have given in – I knew I had no choice.

The Kommandant, now enjoying his moment of glory, detailed a guard to escort me in the direction of the cold water tap which was situated just outside the camp kitchen. Arriving there, those assembled decreed in their wisdom that the problem regarding my filthy clothes could best be resolved by a concentrated hosing down with cold water. Much to my dismay I saw no possible way of declining this ungenerous offer and so there I stood with a rapidly-festering wound on the back of my hand which, up to this moment in time, had stopped bleeding but now, with a sudden cascade of cold water, again started to pour blood.

Stripped of my clothing which was now steam drying by the soup boilers in the kitchen, I was given a thin blanket and told to await the arrival of the French Canadian medical orderly. It turned out to be a vain wait, for he sent word back to say that he had no antiseptic to offer, indeed even his paper bandages had somehow 'disappeared'. I was allowed the whole day in peace – whatever that implied. Being in the camp kitchen I had warmth against the bitter driving wind outside. The 'cooks' gave me a very warming can of soup and had it not been for the thought of Jack lying somewhere quite close by and remembering that only hours ago he had been a living, caring human being, I could, with a little effort, have regarded this present moment in time as pure blissful escapism.

Later that same afternoon, I joined an assembled knot of prisoners who had congregated by the gate to bid a last farewell to Jack. We were silenced to witness his body, still covered by the thin grey blanket, being taken away for burial, unceremoniously pushed along on a builder's handcart.

Immediately after this I was again taken in front of the Kommandant who summarily informed me that a full report of the incident had been sent to higher authority and that I would be advised of my situation in due course. However, within a matter of two or three days, the whole camp was in turmoil. Hell had broken loose: it seemed that the Russians had made yet another unexpected push in our direction, so we were again on the move, hopefully for the last time.

CHAPTER TEN

Dresden – Saxony
Alles Kaput!

Drauskowitz had, in more ways than one, become a refuge, albeit a sad one, but once on the move and with a truly remarkable uplift weather-wise, we were again on our way and heading, or so it was rumoured, towards Czechoslovakia.

This sudden transition from winter to early spring and all in a matter of a few days had lifted morale to new heights. We were still very hungry, very footsore and also still very much lice-infected. My hand was giving some concern, it ached and the area surrounding the wound had developed a pinkish-purple tinge which no one liked the look of.

We walked and walked possibly for three or four days with nothing of interest to relate. We stopped, we slept in barns and we managed, through the persistent foraging of all concerned, to acquire a few potatoes from different farms as we walked along. One distinctive feature lay in the fact that we had taken a route along very minor roads where for hours on end we seldom came across any visible sign of human habitation.

The low muffled rumbling of the distant guns somehow appeared to have bypassed us as we, constantly moving in a south-westerly direction, had now concluded that by whatever means the Russians had taken, we had obviously slipped through the net and at the moment we were moving through an undisputed area of ground to the south of their main thrust into Germany. After our journey over the previous months which had taken us over snow-swept flat and desolate terrain, we were immensely encouraged by the startling change in the landscape. We seemed to be making a steady climb through forests thick and dark, with enormous pine trees at times so tall and dense as to almost completely blot out all natural daylight, before quite suddenly and unexpectedly breaking out into lush green meadows strangely noticeable for their almost complete lack of cattle. It was at this point that we crossed the River Elbe and saw perched up high on a distant craggy mountain a huge fairy-tale castle very similar, we thought, to the pre-war German Tourist Board posters more often seen discoloured and with corners curling with age and the effect of the sun in the window of the local Tommy Cook Travel Agency back home.

One smart-arse in our midst gave the location of that castle as Königstein and went on to tell us that General Giraud, a well-known Frenchman, had escaped, not I suppose without a little help from his friends, but who nevertheless had made a magnificent run, from that very castle to finally finish up serving with the Free French Forces in North Africa.

It was, I remember, that self same evening that we arrived at a very large clearing and, to our amazement, situated right in the centre was a comparatively small, well laid-out but completely uninhabited prison camp. At that time we didn't quite take in the full significance of this magical moment of truth – this was to be our final resting place in captivity. We had huts to sleep in but there was no bedding. We had a camp kitchen but no food and an ironic twist of fate decreed that we had sit-on-a pole type toilets. Indeed, these were an added luxury after months of squatting over latrine pits or having one's exposed backside savagely mangled by the sharp thorns mischievously sited along the uncharitable but conveniently-placed hedgerows. But they were unfortunately woefully short on space as one can imagine with, say, possibly sixty or so anxious customers and only a dozen perches.

We again bunked in together, myself, Jock, Ben, Jeff and Ron. However it was unanimously agreed that bunk beds without any supportive means of comfort or warmth were completely useless, so we set to with a will to break up the wooden frames and start a fire. This, we mistakenly thought, was a truly original act of common sense and initiative unlikely to be thought of by the remainder but, leaving the hut to light our fire outside made us quickly realise we were about the last group to think of it – most of the other syndicates' fires were already blazing away.

Jerry had promised food by the morning and sure enough into the camp came two handcarts loaded with cabbages, potatoes and a small sack of barley. The camp kitchen sprung to life and, with saliva drooling from the corners of our mouths, we patiently stood in line and waited. Afterwards sinking back into a euphoric state of unfamiliar satisfaction, hot potato and cabbage soup with a liberal dose of barley had never tasted so good, we had started to live again. The depression of times past was slowly being dispersed by a much-improved climate and with days very similar to the warm sunny spells we associate with an English summer, a gut feeling that the end of our journey might perhaps be just around the corner and with the unfamiliar experience of an uncomfortably full stomach, a surge of carefree optimism began to spread like a friendly virus throughout the camp.

Maybe it just had to be that kind of day but it had been savoured to the full. We sat around, we dozed a little and talked a lot, not only with our own group but with many others who joined in what turned out to be something of a verbal contest to discover who, if any of us, could claim to have pulled the cheekiest advantage over some unsuspecting victim. I resurrected my oft-repeated version of the German compasses in Tunis but it scarcely raised a flicker of approval. An Aussie, present for the first time in our illustrious gathering, reminded us, indeed quite painfully for some, of the obsessive preoccupation of his fellow countrymen to relieve we British of our cap badges.

Most of the Aussies who had been stationed in Egypt went about sporting wide leather belts generously studded with the cap badges belonging to a large number of British Regiments in a similar manner, we suspected, to the way the Red Indians once collected scalps. Now, we each had one cap badge and one only. Losing possession of this badge usually meant a charge brought under Section 40 paragraph something or other of the Army Act of being improperly dressed and this could have dire consequence for the unfortunate concerned. The Australians knew of this and knew that if they wished to acquire a badge, then the only solution open to them was to steal it. Their usual method of performing was to lurk with an accomplice, seated at a table by the door of a cafe or bar, and wait for an unsuspecting victim to present himself. The more seasoned campaigners were fully aware of this subterfuge but newcomers to the Middle East, easily recognisable by their white arms and legs, were the natural prey of the Aussies.

A mock argument would break out between the two Aussies who, in loud tones, would pretend to differ on the point as to whether or not the newcomer, blissfully unaware at this stage of the part he himself was about to play, had a lion or some similarly arguable feature on his cap badge. Then, in an apparent move to settle the disagreement, one of the Aussies would drift over and quite politely ask if he could perhaps borrow the chap's cap for a couple of seconds to prove that the cap badge had or had not got a lion on it.

Eager to oblige, the newcomer would willingly offer his cap and badge for inspection leaving the Aussies free to dash out of the bar with yet another scalp for their belt.

Several of those present could be seen ruefully shaking their heads. They had not only heard it all before – they'd experienced it!

Our discussion group was attracting a lot of attention and many other acts of minor villainy were beginning to get an airing. One old chestnut, that of repacking dried tea leaves and selling them at an inflated price to the Arabs was greeted with some derision, whilst a certain amount of credit was given to the many who frequently laboured through their hours of rest filling small sand bags with some of the inexhaustible supply of sand Tunisia had to offer and then selling it off to the always impressionable American servicemen at an astronomical price as a bag of genuine El Alamein sand!

True, Napoleon was once reputed to have said that we were a nation of shopkeepers although, having heard of the many deeds perpetrated against the innocents with possibly after all, a few minor incursions of my own in that field, we would perhaps have been better described as a nation of musicians (fiddlers).

The following morning, during roll-call, we were called upon to volunteer to help clear the damage created by a series of heavy bombing raids on the nearby city of Dresden. This was unfortunate because nobody had any intention whatsoever of expending even one ounce of energy in favour of the Jerry. I say it was unfortunate because, having had no sudden surge of takers for this plum job, the whole front rank, myself included, was summarily deemed to have volunteered by silence. Not only is it jokingly said of the Germans that they 'Haf vays of making you talk', they also have ways of making you volunteer!

What we were to witness, however, was a complete eye-opener. We had been transported under guard to Dresden, perched precariously balanced on the back of two antiquated charcoal burning trucks and our first view of this devastated city seen from a distance of several miles was undeniably one of sheer incredulity. Very little appeared to be left standing and the closer we got, the more extensive seemed the damage. The whole area was absolutely devastated. Civilians roamed around, I thought, very much like the totally demented inmates walking around the grounds of a secure Mental Home. No one paid the slightest heed to us. Civilian and military police were everywhere. One could easily forget that the actual devastation of Dresden had taken place between 13th and 16th February and yet to ourselves, the onlookers, the damage was so fresh, if that is the word, as to have happened but yesterday. We moved carefully, avoiding mounds of rubble, buildings whose walls were leaning precariously at a tortured and listless angle, and gaping fissures snaking haphazardly where the roads had been partially cleared and were accessible only to allow limited pedestrian access.

Salvage squads were still trying to recover the dead trapped deep in the heart of the rubble. The stench was pretty horrific and no doubt word had gone out to seek and destroy the rotting bodies in order to prevent a possible epidemic.

Close to where we were ordered to halt, stood what had, until recently, been a parade of small shops. One badly damaged but still recognisable unit had been a butcher's shop, now crippled and desolate with a gaping eyeless socket where the window had once been and with a weary looking facia sign dejectedly advertising the business as a one time 'Fleischerei' hanging drunkenly at an angle, mournfully and reluctantly accepting its complete and untimely demise.

We had rather hoped that, having been pressed into the dubious role of 'volunteers', we might well get lucky and find ourselves sorting out someone's hurriedly-vacated pantry, but a glance over the road at a point very close to where the butcher's shop had been, brought into focus an unusually ornate street lamp listing badly in its foundations and, suspended from the top arm was the decaying body of a man.

Two members of our party — I didn't know them — morbidly attracted by this dangling corpse, edged closer to read the wording on the card which had been placed around

the neck of the dead man. To their great consternation –
and ours – we learned that the man had been hanged as a
looter. This revelation quelled our recent impulse to partake
in a healthy spot of looting.

Our guards, detailed to present us for salvage work, were
having little success in finding a willing employer. As can be
imagined there was a tremendous need for help but the lia-
bility of closely supervising a gang of unwilling prisoners such
as we, far outweighed any possible advantage. For instance,
we could not be allowed to wander around indiscriminately,
that would have resulted in a deficiency of numbers at roll
call, and collectively we stood to get in the way of people
wanting to help. So, rather reluctantly, we were ordered to
start a fire and burn as much rubbish and wood as possible.
This we did with a will. We tossed bits of wood onto a raging
fire and tried hard to forget that so far that day we had
had neither food nor drink. We strove to make it a social,
leisurely day and on our return to the camp shortly before
dusk, we were delighted to be given the news that an issue
of biscuits and soup would be made within the hour. The
idea of recruiting people like ourselves to assist the Germans,
desperately in need of a miracle to lift them out of the mire,
was a lost cause. We were never again sent to Dresden.

When one comes to think of it, an ordinary civilian prisoner
doing time in an ordinary jail is made fully aware of his
situation. He knows when he goes in exactly how long he
will be there, he eats comparatively well, he knows what is
happening on the outside world and in other words, although
closely confined in a place of detention, he is still able to
enjoy the benefits of an orderly existence. In retrospect I
frequently wonder how people such as ourselves managed to
retain our sanity. Apart from the deprivation of the facilities
mentioned, I personally had managed to send home one
card briefly stating that 'I was well', during the whole of
my captivity. I had received no mail, not even a postcard,
in fact, communication-wise, we were living in a complete
vacuum. The only news we received, sketchy as it was, came
via the German propaganda machine, as usual threatening the
complete and utter annihilation of our country as we knew
it. The bombs, the V.1s and V.2s, we had heard of. Rumour
had it that all our major towns and cities had been razed to
the ground by these new weapons designed, we were told,

to extract full and exact retribution for the wanton damage inflicted on the German nation by the Allied, 'Terror Flieges', as the joint airforces were known, and indeed, for several weeks past – no news at all! An air raid by the Americans had taken place on some none-too-distant target only the other day and a crippled Fortress struggling unsuccessfully to gain height had crashed only a few miles away from where we had helplessly stood. It was a sad sight and an undignified end to a fine aircraft and a courageous crew.

Recounting happenings such as the matter of a dog may seem quite incredible to the uninformed but, starting at the beginning, which took place on the day of our abortive aid session in Dresden, someone had picked up a small mongrel pup sniffing around the ruins and, without even considering how one could keep even a small dog without the necessary means of support, the animal was nevertheless spirited back into the camp hidden underneath someone's jacket. The dog was allowed to roam freely around the hut where we lived but it was unable due to its tender age to provide for itself by chasing the odd mouse or rat and we, as I have said, were totally unable to offer anything. Food had again become a problem, no longer had we the makings of a fine soup such as we had until quite recently managed on a fairly regular basis, and therefore, with many a lean and hungry look, we now began to look towards our dog as a future means of sustenance. An emergency meeting was convened with the prime intention of nominating an honorary butcher who would be delegated to humanely dispose of the poor creature whose mortal remains would then be consigned to the cooking pot. Looking down at the pathetic wispy hind quarters of the dog, its tiny tail gently wagging, at peace with the world and completely unaware that its small carcass was the subject of our earnest conversation, I suddenly realised that my gripping hunger pains had miraculously evaporated and that for my money, the pup's sweetbreads had become inviolable.

The discussion was rapidly becoming more heated and seriously aggravated by the emotive issues involved. 'Were we,' we began to ask ourselves 'a nation of dog lovers or a nation of dog eaters?' However, whatever the outcome may have been we shall never know as the prevailing uproar became suddenly muted at the sound of a rifle shot. Our immediate thought was that some unfortunate had thoughtlessly strayed too close to the trip wire and had been shot. Rushing out to join the crowd hastily gathering around the back of the huts we were temporarily shocked to find the body of a German sentry lying sprawled out on the ground with half his head blown away, and even in death, still clutching his rifle.

So far, we had felt that most of the pressures and despair had centred around us, but here lying before us, was the proof that even the enemy's armour was beginning to show a few cracks. Speculation was rife when immediately following this incident, a call went out summoning everyone to a special parade, and having assembled we were again to witness the enfolding of yet another of life's rich tapestries.

The Kommandant, escorted by his senior N.C.O.s, moved slowly towards the centre of the scene. The next move was reminiscent of a badly-performed conjuring trick when suddenly, on a signal from the Kommandant, several guards came into the camp each bearing a huge cardboard box.

These boxes were quickly opened and on a given command their contents, namely packets of 20 cigarettes and packets of Knäckebrot biscuits were distributed amongst us. The first thought immediately to spring to mind was one of suspicion: talk about the 'Beware the Greeks bearing gifts' adage. Was this to be a sugar-coated pill to allay new fears or was the Jerry going plain soft on us?

Having carried out this wholesale distribution of largesse in a dramatically self-conscious and mind-boggling fashion, we didn't pause to work out any further permutations otherwise we would have been obliged to remember that here were the guards – the enemy – handing out to us all the things that they themselves were deprived of. At this point we saw the Man-of-Confidence mount a hastily-erected platform and immediately commence to address us. Normally he would have taken a very secondary place in the pecking order with that order of seniority being taken right down to the lowest-ranking member of the German detachment. This in itself could only be something to our advantage as indeed it was. The war was over. We were free but – and there was a big but – it appeared that the Russians were still in the immediate area trying to settle a longstanding difference of opinion with a Waffen S.S. Division which was holding out and flatly refusing to accept what was now a foregone conclusion, namely that the war was at an end.

In a nutshell, it was put to us that the nearest 'friendly' allies were the American forces, now estimated to have advanced as far as Karlsbad which lay in Czechoslovakia approximately 80 or so miles south west of our present position. In order to reach them it was suggested that the guards should retain their weapons as a means of protection against marauding bands of recently-liberated prisoners of many nationalities, the Russians and also the still-predatory German S.S. troops.

From our late captors' point of view it was pretty obvious that they hoped to gain a moral advantage by handing us over to the Americans, whereby they would hopefully expect to be granted a safe passage back into the western part of occupied Germany. A vote taken on this issue indicated that the majority of us were in favour of this plan and, for my part, it would enable me on our contacting the Americans to point the finger at the guard who had shot Jack, to my way of thinking quite callously and unnecessarily, and also to obtain some retribution for the damage done to my hand.

Quite quickly and with scarcely a backwards glance, we left what had been our resting place for the past few days. Our dog had mysteriously disappeared, as well as the body of the dead guard killed by his own hand and they, along with whatever other memories we might have had, were left behind us as we set off to cover the remaining distance between this miserable country and hopefully soon our own people. Trudging through the foothills of the Südaten mountains on a bright and very warm sunny day left us feeling full of eager anticipation in respect of the future, a feeling so intense as to completely obliterate the usually obsessive self-torturing and endless conversation revolving around food. Hungry we were, but we now had a goal to aim for — the Americans.

Spurred on by the angry sounds of a nearby skirmish — lots of rifle and automatic fire with an occasional outburst of shelling, we began to see more clearly how we were cautiously threading our way through what must be this last contested piece of ground. Frantic movement of troops, scowling, evil-looking men, some clad in their traditional black uniforms, others in ordinary field grey, were seen dotted at intervals along our path — maybe, we thought, our tame German escort was standing us in good stead after all. As we continued to walk through their lines some, more truculent than others, shouted abuse at us whilst the remainder either stared balefully or simply chose to ignore us.

The urge to be free had now become paramount and forgetting all else we continued our walk, pausing only for a brief rest every hour or so. Towards dusk however, we really began to feel the pace of the day's events — so much so that several of us, myself included, actually fell asleep whilst still walking. This led to an occasional outburst of peevish bickering because as the pace sometimes slackened, those of us who had dropped off to sleep often found ourselves bumping into the people in front of us or tripping up those walking behind. A short period of excitement followed when two Russian aircraft patrolling the area spotted us and, mistaking us for an enemy troop movement, made a couple of runs straffing us as they passed at a very low level without inflicting a single casualty. It seemed doubly annoying to be shot at after hostilities had presumably ceased, but to be straffed by one's supposed allies was an even greater affront to one's dignity!

Someone estimated that we must have covered at least twenty or so miles since leaving our last camp and the pace was really beginning to tell. Word passed down the column to the effect that we were now moving across the border with Czechoslovakia, giving some stimulus to our rapidly tiring legs, and it was with a feeling of sheer relief that we were brought to a halt on a scrub-covered hillside where we were given the glad tidings that here we would rest up for the night and hopefully make contact with the Americans sometime the following day.

Sleeping on a chilly hillside with no real means of keeping warm may have presented a problem but we were far too exhausted to worry over such trivialities. We were tired and we slept, in fact we slept far too soundly and never heard a sound as the Germans — our late captors, obviously acting on a pre-conceived plan — disappeared, lock, stock and barrel. Admittedly on reflection they had done very little towards getting us through to our present position: we had not eaten, granted, we had our dwindling supply of cigarettes to thank them for but we still felt that we had been let down.

CHAPTER ELEVEN

Teplitz – Brüx – Karlsbad

Red Cross – Red Army

Sluggishly we began to stir and stretch our aching limbs and, as if by some unspoken decision, now that the Germans had left, we began to wander off in small groups towards what we believed was that part of Czechoslovakia now occupied by the American forces.

Jock and I decided to go it alone and set off with the prime intention of finding a farm or some similar habitation which might provide us with a meal. To our way of thinking this was by far the most sensible move as, with all the will in the world, we couldn't go on using up our energy through walking without at least taking on board a few calories.

Many people had stayed behind still resting and unable to decide their next move. Others had pushed rapidly ahead and, apart from the odd isolated group ploughing its lonely furrow in a similar direction to ours, we were pretty much on our own when suddenly, a rather strange, at first unidentifiable noise, could be heard quite some distance away but steadily approaching us from the rear. Shortly afterwards, as the clamour increased, we were surprised to see, moving slowly towards us, a long well-spaced-out column of horse-drawn carts headed by an extremely antiquated truck which must surely have been, I would imagine, pre-first world war vintage. Never at a loss to exploit a potentially material gain, we raised our hands expectantly, signalling the driver to stop. The driver, shabbily dressed in his light brown uniform and with an oversized cap bearing a huge red star, stared down balefully from what seemed a tremendous height. The convoy, shunted to a halt by the slow braking of the truck, stood patiently waiting with their loads of animal fodder perched precariously high and unsecured on each flat-bottomed dray.

As he looked down on us with a strange quizzical look on his flat features, Jock, gazing upwards, declared in his broadest Scottish accent that we were 'Angelski' and that we would like a cigarette. The dawn of realisation appeared to surface on the Russian's features and pointing at each of us in turn he repeated the word 'Angelski'? Imagine our consternation and surprise when, with a quick and totally unexpected response, he leaned out of the cab and spat on us. Jock, always ready to make light of an awkward situation simply said, 'Thank God he's one of ours!'

After this shaft of enlightenment, we decided to break off along a secondary road which seemed to lead towards a small village visible about two miles or so distant from where we were. This turned out to be a lucky – or perhaps unlucky – encounter with two Belgian forced labourers.

We came to the village, a desolate, drab place comprising of a conglomeration of ugly and time-ravaged buildings which, apart from ourselves and a Belgian couple, appeared to be completely deserted. Quickly explaining their situation in German, they explained how, as a married couple, they had been forcibly transported to Czechoslovakia where they were set to work following their normal peacetime occupation as bakers, working from this village and supplying the surrounding area, which was inhabited in the main by Südeten Germans, with a regular supply of bread.

Only on the day previous had the German Bürgermeister decreed that the entire population of the village should evacuate before the arrival of the Russians. Asking for bread, we were delighted to be each given a one and a half kilo loaf by our Belgian benefactors and, elated beyond belief by our sudden good fortune, we headed off to the welcoming comfort of a nearby barn and, sinking rapturously into the welcoming straw, we began to take apart our huge and still warm from the oven bread.

That to us was the good news but the bad news, quick to follow, came in the shape of violent stomach cramps. Unused to such munificent patronage, our poor old shrunken stomachs could not cope with this sudden and excessive influx of food. Almost unable to move, we were to remain in this uncomfortable state for the next thirty-six to forty-eight hours, and although when the worst had passed we were able to laugh about it, I must confess that it was pretty debilitating at the time.

Before leaving, the Belgians had told us that rumour had it that the Soviets had occupied the part of Czechoslovakia that we were passing through and that hordes of them were running amok, killing, raping and pillaging as they felt fit. The Americans, they thought, had stopped short at Karlsbad, a town possibly fifty miles south west of our present position and much further afield than we had originally thought, and they suggested that we double back to the main road and turn left towards a small town named Brüx which boasted a rail link with Karlsbad.

Bidding a final farewell to them, we gradually made our way back to the main road which was by this time in a chaotic state. Refugees moving in our direction consisted in the main of Südeten Germans: men, women and children, pushing their moveable belongings on small wooden hand carts or struggling along with backpacks, suitcases and children of all ages. At this stage little was seen of the Russians but as we moved along in the main stream of humanity surging along the overcrowded road, we noticed that the general pace was slackening until we at last came to a grinding halt.

The reason for the hold-up gradually became very clear. It appeared that the Belgians had been right in what they said about the Ruskies. Road blocks had been set up ahead at intervals of possibly two or three hundred metres and the demoralised Germans, running the gauntlet of each successive obstruction, were to suffer unimaginable humiliation and worse at the hands of their tormentors. Anything, even items of little use to anyone, were being taken from them. Men, regardless of age, were being physically beaten and robbed whilst the women, both young and old, were being subjected to all manner of degradation with many young mothers still pathetically clutching their small children whilst being raped by the roadside.

These Russians appeared to be of an exceptionally low standard of intellect, with their flat vacant faces and shabby uniforms, many in a drunken state acting so completely out of control as to make one wonder whether or not this was just a part of a very unpleasant nightmare. I still feel that we were lucky to get through this demented mob without injury. Their lack of intelligence made it an exceedingly difficult task for them to understand that we were English, but for some unaccountable reason they obviously sensed that even in our semi-emaciated state and with worn out and dirty clothing, we were somehow different from the civilian refugees. Walking along the road towards home, with a warm breeze on our backs and a clear blue sky above was, I thought, tragically in conflict with all that was going on about us and, stirred by a sharp premonition, I couldn't help but wonder if, after six years away from home, what we were witnessing was going to be the sum total of it all.

Surely, I considered, if these people were really the winners, then what hope were the losers left to cling to. We had of course no news of what was happening on the other side of Germany where our own troops had been fighting, or indeed how it was intended to get people like ourselves repatriated or, even more to the point, how we would, in post-war Europe, manage to cope with the necessity of living with our Russian friends. All we could do was to keep walking in the hope that eventually something would happen to happily expedite our safe return home. It had, as I said, been a glorious day. The roads were still very heavily congested with refugees who, with the same monotonous regularity, were still being persecuted by the vindictive actions of the Ruskies, although as the distance lengthened the smaller became the amount of loot available for collection, although this, however, did not altogether deter these flat-faced villains who had now set about stripping the clothing from those refugees who, until this time, had managed to cling on to a few modest garments. Late afternoon saw us still in the middle of this chaotic exodus to nowhere and again we decided to leave the main road in search of shelter for the night. Jock, pointing to a side road, reasoned that if it was worth a road, be it all but a cart track, then there must be something at the end of it and sure enough, after covering a few short miles, we came across a somewhat larger than usual farmhouse. Approaching the farmhouse and finding the stable-type door wide open, we entered the kitchen only to find one hell of a shambles.

Obviously and without doubt the Ruskies had left their visiting card. The whole house, we were to discover, had been systematically pillaged and vandalised not once, we imagined, but several times. Broken china, furniture and most appalling of all, the human excrement covering the floor of every room. The stench was absolutely revolting and we made a quick sprint back to the fresh air. Adding to our complete bewilderment, we paused at the muffled sounds of a baby crying. The noise appeared to have come from the direction of a barn situated at the rear and some distance from the farmhouse but, wherever it had originated we now had nothing other than an eerie silence.

In retrospect, it may now seem absurd to confess to a sense of bewilderment but that was exactly what we were experiencing. It was again all turning into a dream-like existence. My hand, still badly festering, was aching, as was my stomach. My feet were blistered and my toes were still showing the after-effects of a slight attack of frostbite. Knee joints were swollen with what was later diagnosed as beri-beri, a vitamin deficiency disease and, coupled with hunger, fatigue and body lice, one could scarcely be criticized for feeling slightly out of alignment.

However, we were determined to prove to ourselves, I suppose, that we had not in fact been hallucinating as we softly made our way over to where we first suspected the sound of a baby's cry had been heard. Entering the barn had the same effect as entering a dark cavern. Nothing could be seen until our eyes had grown accustomed to the dim surroundings and sure enough we again heard the faint muffled sound of a baby crying and this time we were able to locate the exact direction of the noise.

Wading through the thickly piled straw we slowly made our way to the far left hand corner of the barn, and there, huddled together absolutely petrified with fright, lay two women, one of whom was clutching a tiny child in her arms. Our first assumption proved correct, it was in fact a mother, daughter and grand-daughter all, as we thought, German, lying half hidden and waiting apprehensively for our next move.

We smiled at them and Jock (at first glance not a very pretty sight) lapsed into his familiar Scottish/German patois assuring them that we were Engländers and intended no harm. Relunctant at first to respond, the elder woman gradually began to thaw out, timidly giving way to Jock's gentle efforts to put them at their ease. Their tale, perfectly true, I feel sure, was not a very happy story, but we had of late developed a total immunity against happy endings and their story was just another sad repetition of what seemed to be happening all over this part of Europe.

The husband of the older woman had died leaving her to run this rather large farm as best she could. The daughter later married a serving member of the German Kriegsmarine and then, since her husband had been taken prisoner in Denmark, moved in with her small baby to help out with the running of the farm.

For the past few nights the whole area had been systematically pillaged by marauding bands of drunken Russians who had either driven away or slaughtered all the livestock, razed to the ground several outbuildings and, having completely vandalised the house, had retained what was left of it as a drinking den much in use during their nightly orgies. Both women had suffered the indignity of being raped several times by them during their initial onslaught on the farm and were unwilling to relinquish their slightly more tenable position here instead of running the gauntlet through the Ruskies, more or less permanently stationed along the main road. The women had noticed that, for some unaccountable reason, the Russians seldom put in an appearance during the day, and it was only towards nightfall that they unerringly returned to create futher havoc upon the already decimated buildings. Necessity and practice compelled the women to return to the kitchen during the day and hurriedly prepare a meal of barley and potatoes from the scant stock which they had managed to hide. 'Would you,' they asked, 'like us to prepare a similar meal for you?' Thankfully we accepted but hastened to point out that as dusk was already beginning to fall, they must hurry and we would accompany them to the farmhouse.

Food for the baby presented no real problem as the mother was still feeding her herself and later, sitting in the barn, well hidden away from the eyes of any likely predator, we felt the tension rising in the nervous movements of the two women. It must have been towards midnight before we witnessed the arrival of those strange, almost animal-like, ill-disciplined band of drunken looters who even then were noisy and already quarrelling amongst themselves as they commenced to deliberately set fire to the farmhouse they had so severely damaged over the preceding nights.

Silhouetted against the burning backdrop, prancing up and down like demented demons from Hell, we were aware that these people acting so badly in a so-called liberated country would undoubtedly act in a similar fashion if ever they were to over-run the rest of Europe. Fighting together against a common enemy as we had done was one thing but co-existing with them, we believed, would be an entirely different matter.

Chilled, I suppose by shock rather than by the cold night air, we retired to our hollowed-out bunker in the straw, the more to obliterate from our thoughts what was happening out there than to savour the hope of a good night's sleep.

Lying closely huddled together with the women and child, we gained a little from the communal warmth of human contact, but we were fearful to doze in case the Ruskies should decide to concentrate their attentions on the barn we were lying in. I suppose that to date Jock and I had been very lucky indeed to escape the aggressive attentions of our drink-besotted allies.

Jock, habitually strutting around with his normal slightly aggressive and provocative attitude well to the fore, no doubt went some way towards confusing the thoughts and any possible suspicion the Ruskies may have had, but how much further our luck was likely to extend was a matter of pure conjecture. Thoughts such as these crossed my mind many times during that long night but towards dawn the noise of revelry and shooting had died down, giving us hope that perhaps we might soon be once more on our way.

This was in fact the case. The enormous blazing remains that had once been a farmhouse were slowly dying down, the Ruskies appeared to have departed and we prepared to bid our farewell to the German women who were now openly weeping and pleading to be allowed to accompany us through to the American lines. Reluctantly we had to refuse as to be encumbered with them would result in a drastic reduction in our pace which had already slowed down far below our expectations.

There was also the fact that although we could hopefully continue to move fairly freely through the road blocks, there was always a chance that our present freedom of movement could be drastically curtailed were we to be seen in the company of two German women and a child. No, we decided, compassion was a luxury that, on this occasion anyhow, must be thrown overboard. We advised them to stay where they were and hope that once the overall position became a little more stabilised, there might well be a chance of their being repatriated to Germany.

Making our way back to the main road with the sun already beginning to warm our aching bones, we somehow felt more optimistic than of late. And why not?: we were heading in a general direction which we hoped would eventually lead us to the Yanks; the war, we knew, was over and as a parting gift the women had given us a small canvas bag of barley and a few cold baked potatoes to share. The road was as thronged as ever with thousands of refugees, hordes of Ruskies and a countless number of horse-drawn carts. Goodness knows what had happened to the highly mechanised units of the Soviet army!

We tried hard but with little success to blank out from our minds all that was happening about us – this very morning we had witnessed several men beaten quite callously and unnecessarily into the ground. Maybe it was the shock of being close at hand when these things happened, but from the Russian point of view, bearing in mind what the Germans had done in Russia, in their eyes retribution was rightfully theirs. What we were being forced to witness was, to say the least, completely un-British but whilst deploring the actions of the Ruskies, we wondered if, on the liberation of our country from an oppressor as violent and as ruthless as the Germans had been, would we have acted so differently to the Russians? – I doubt it.

Pushing on as best we could we eventually passed through a small town named Teplitz, a town which, although well inside the Czechoslovak border, still bore every sign of its, until quite recent, occupation by the Germans as part of the Südetenland. A quick glance around as we passed through made us again long for the more wholesome nature of the open countryside. Drunken Russian soldiers were everywhere although, to be fair, we counted more lying on the ground in an ugly drunken stupor than otherwise engaged in breaking the plate glass windows of small shops and encouraging the local populace to loot their meagre contents. Why, I don't know. Out of the few pathetic shop units being attacked, I only saw one with any goods on display and even this shop, a shoe shop, sported nothing more than a few clumsily cobbled shoes with wooden soles.

Most welcome of all, however, was a soup kitchen which had been set up in a rather old fashioned type of building reminiscent, in a way, of the age-grimmed and depressing town halls found in the northern industrial towns of England. Hordes of recently released forced labourers from almost every country in Europe thronged this huge hall clamouring for food. A group of perhaps ten or so British ex-P.O.W.s had skillfully elbowed their way to the front of the queue and upon catching sight of us called out an invitation to join them.

This we did and the rather startling feature was that no one in the queue registered any objection. Cabbage soup thickened with oatmeal, a hunk of bread and a small mug of acorn coffee turned out to be a meal fit for a king. No one paused to wonder where this splendid generous donation of food came from and more to the point, nobody cared.

Encouraged to rest a while and later on to make yet another onslaught on the soup kitchen was an offer one just could not resist. Outside, the hungry stream of silent German refugees slipped by, anxious not to raise the anger of the Russian soldiery, seriously intent on drinking anything from, one would imagine, pure wood alcohol to engine oil, indulging in the odd brawl, chasing some unfortunate wench or, more common than not, lying stupified due to their own excesses in a pool of vomit.

By one means or another, Jock and I were in complete agreement that we must go along with the rumour that the Americans had moved as far as Karlsbad and, by agreement with the Soviets, had decided to accept this position as part of the demarcation line between the two armies. We had seemingly become a lesser part of society now that war was over than when we were caged up. The Russians were making it very obvious that they didn't want to know. We had at first optimistically wondered if the Soviets might take steps to repatriate us but any such hope had been rudely dashed by their attitude of complete indifference towards our situation. It seemed at the time an easy way out just to stay put and let things take a natural course, however we were very much against any further period of inactivity and we decided to get out of Teplitz and again make for the countryside and a barn with a plentiful supply of welcoming straw in which to bed down and get off the following morning to a good start.

On our second day out of Teplitz we came across a small party of chaps who had been with us since the time at Waldenstein. They were in high spirits, having just turned over the contents of an extremely large country house hidden from the main road by a thick screen of poplars. Giving us the story as they saw it, it was pretty certain that this house had been taken over by someone very senior in the Nazi hierarchy who had evidently looted and plundered his way through a series of occupied countries, and the entire fruits of his labour had apparently come to rest in this rather sedate and fortress-like residence in Czechoslovakia.

Anticipating the coming of the Russians and moving out hastily ahead of lots of Germans lower down in the pecking order, they had been unable to move off with their ill-gotten gains and evidently, according to our friends, the whole lot was up for grabs. Looking back to that time we must have presented a truly incongruous sight as we staggered about heavily laden with such valuable items as solid silver candelabra, ornate clocks, priceless Meissen figurines and possibly invaluable paintings brilliantly executed and mounted in highly-decorated bronze frames. All this, if you can imagine, a veritable treasure house of Europe and we, lice-ridden, dirty and down-at-heel in full albeit temporary possession of it all.

I tried to choose wisely although with scant knowledge of such works of art, it made a daunting task. Bearing in mind that we were not in an altogether fit state to carry heavy articles over a possibly long distance, I decided to settle for a rather large but not too weighty leather bound and securely padlocked stamp collection.

Being, I suppose, a Philistine at heart, I had broken the lock of the album and not knowing the value of the contents, but appreciating the fact that if their former owner had considered them worth pillaging, assumed they must carry a fairly substantial price tag. What a euphoric state we were experiencing, the weather was perfect, we were on our way home and − if our luck held out − we, or most of us, had the wherewithal to become comparatively rich.

Little wonder that we set off down the road secure in the belief that for us the future held nothing but the best. To this day I cannot remember what Jock decided to 'liberate' from that house but I distinctly remember trundling along that long highway with my recently-acquired album uncomfortably secured across my back with a piece of also recently 'borrowed' rope. Many times along that road I was to surreptitiously glance at the Russian soldiers still steadfastly manning their road blocks, blindly seeking the kind of wealth that we had hopefully taken possession of.

Uneducated and sadly unappreciative as we were of the better things in life, the Russians were even less aware. The clouded judgement of these Slavic entrepreneurs seemed to extend very little further than in the acquisition of a more substantial tally of wrist watches than that of their confederates, all of whom took a fiendish delight in removing timepieces from the wrists of anyone naive enough to sport one. My backpack of postage stamps thankfully failed to stimulate anything more than an occasional disinterested glance.

The road was unbearably uncomfortable to walk on. We had several times been driven off it so that the Soviet convoys could move up and down. We still had the problem of the refugee columns so dense at times as to repeatedly force us off the road in order to gain some headway and, of course, we had the roadblocks. Approaching each block in turn we had now mastered the art of subterfuge, and would simply walk round the obstacle rather than queueing to pass through it and muttering to any challenging Russian that we were 'Angelski'. But, as everything has an ending, we too had ours and, with a sigh of relief, we had come to the end, although at this stage we didn't know it, of our walk which had taken so very long to accomplish – we had finally arrived at the Czechoslovakian Spa town of Brüx.

CHAPTER TWELVE
Pilsen
Yanks, homeward bound

Our unheralded arrival in this once-upon-a-time sleepy spa town could scarcely have been said to have brought about a surge of frenzied hysteria from the inhabitants. The whole place it seemed was threatening to burst at the seams with a positively seething mass of humanity drawn from almost every country in Europe and the added inclusion of two more odd-balls optimistically craving the sight of a friendly face was, to say the least, decidedly unlikely to create even a ripple of excitement.

Jock, his infinite wisdom prevailing as per usual, recommended the Town Hall as a possible source of both food and information and, reluctant to challenge his judgement, although his suggestion still caused me to wonder if for some unknown reason – possibly, though jokingly, due to a deprived childhood or some other deficiency – he had a remarkable hang-up on Town Halls.

Now I personally did not wish in any way to concern myself with the beauty, functioning and so forth of these establishments although according to Jock, Scotland seemed to be over-run with them. Anecdotes concerning his pre-war brushes with authority appeared to centre around his full-scale war with the troglodyte-like denizens of these Town Halls all of whom he either challenged or was challenged by on every conceivable point of civic bureaucracy purely, as he so aptly put it, as a 'point of order'. The whole thing was moving in a circular direction I thought as we cast ourselves forward in what was hopefully the direction of the Rathaus. Our quest did not take long and we found ourselves in a small cobbled square totally overpowered by the ostentatious facade of the civic building, unashamedly proclaiming, it seemed, a glory that never was, but now joyfully relishing its liberation in a manner that would no doubt be talked of by the locals for so many years to come. Flags festooned the entire frontage: Russian, Czechoslovakian, home-made American and British flags — indeed we suspected the authenticity of flags which might well have been purposely invented solely on account of the varied selection of bright colours. Pushing past groups of idle onlookers, we made our way inside where Jock, his eyes lighting on a drably uniformed attendant demanded, in German, that we be taken immediately to the Bürgermeister. For a short five foot three chap with a load of nerve sufficient to usually manage to come up smelling of roses is one thing, but in a place like this riddled with both Czech and Russian administrators and plus, of course a liberal bevy of minor bureaucrats, it was little short of a miracle to find ourselves ushered without further ado into the Bürgermeister's chambers.

Having been invited to sit down, we were very favourably impressed by our new acquaintance who immediately began the conversation by informing us that we were the first ever 'English' people to be entertained in his chambers. This declaration was evidently a prelude for what was to follow. A huge bowl of apples, three glasses and a bottle of some rather peculiarly-flavoured spirit were ceremoniously placed on the table after being brought from a huge ornately-carved cupboard which occupied most of the wall facing the huge extinct fireplace. We all three imbibed several rather over-generous measures of the Bürgermeister's brew before he suddenly noticed the state of my hand which was, by this time, looking decidedly unpleasant, and he straight away called for some on-the-spot treatment. This resulted in my being painfully, but at the same time solicitously cared for, by an extraordinarily pretty nurse with fair hair, a sparkling white uniform and a huge red cross emblazoned across her chest.

As a final gesture of goodwill, we were invited to suffer a conducted tour of this rather austere building and so, feeling immensely fortified by our recent drinking session and doubly stimulated by the natural spontaneous friendliness of our host, we readily accepted his offer in the same spirit. Entering one heavily padlocked room we were astounded to behold an Aladdin's Cave filled, almost to bursting point, with confiscated German weaponry. Our Czech host, eager to express still further his warm and unselfconscious generosity,

invited us to take any single item of our choice from the wide
array of captured equipment as a personal souvenir. There were
Lugers, Mausers, and Italian Beretta pistols, Spandau machine
guns, dress swords and bayonets and a host of other things.
Impressed, but at the same time itching to leave, I selected the
nearest item to hand − a Nazi dress bayonet complete with its
frog whilst Jock, also keen to be on the move, chose a Luger
pistol, brand new and still in a coating of grease and loosely
wrapped in a sheet of brown, oily, greaseproof paper.

We bid a fond farewell to our host who, uttering a final
word of warning, advised us that the Russians had been seen
rounding up people like ourselves and placing them in a former
small secure prison camp that had been erected by the railway
sidings on the outskirts of the town and used to house prisoners
in transit.

Being young and inexperienced enough to remain steadfast
in our belief that one should on a point of obstinacy always
ignore advice and do one's own thing, we blithely went along
our way − but not for long. We had been given the location
of a communal soup kitchen and, even before we had a chance
to draw our first bowl of soup, we were intercepted by a patrol
of uncommonly sober Russians who, with the aid of mime,
demanded to know our nationality.

I suppose, quite quickly for them, they established the fact
that we were Angelskis and, without further ceremony, we
were taken under escort to the camp that we had been warned
against. This was, we could see, an offer it would be inadvisable
to refuse and so, depressing as it was, we were quickly carted
off to join a select company of several prisoners of varying
nationalities, none of whom it appeared could admit to having
been fed by the Russians since they were put in the camp.

The accepted drill, we were to learn, was to hang around
the camp wire and await the friendly attentions of the Czech
civilians who, whenever possible, would generously bombard
us with a mixed supply of bread, apples and even cabbages and
potatoes. Several of our old acquaintances had been spotted in
the camp and we spent a lot of our time listening to their tales.
One rather sad event which we heard of concerned two of the
chaps we had known way back from our days at Klimontow.

It was sheer bad luck that led them to a house similar by all
accounts to the one where I had picked up my stamp album but,
unfortunately for them, they had found their way to the kitchen

and eaten, amongst other things, Knäckebrot crispbread, cheese and tinned fish and then, still searching, they had come across a large jar of pickled gherkins. The one chap, I've forgotten his name, was the first to remove the cap off the jar and take out a gherkin. No sooner had he taken a bite than he fell dead at the feet of his friend. The contents had, it was suspected, been laced with cyanide.

When, we began to wonder, would we ever get home? The war must have finished at least two weeks previously and yet we were still here, frustratingly unable to communicate with a friendly face. I suppose however that all things come to an end and sure enough, though Heaven knows how it happened, into the camp, shortly after our arrival, came a small motorised delegation of Swiss Red Cross representatives. Their presence certainly gave a terrific boost to the morale of the entire camp particularly as we were all given a small canvas bag of goodies each containing a packet of cigarettes, sweets, soap and, most welcome of all, a safety razor and, believe it or not, a packet of de-lousing powder!

The Swiss officials told us that it was possible that negotiations for our transfer to the American Sector would be completed within the next few days and that with a bit of luck we could be on our way home very shortly. This was the best piece of news we had received since being told that the war was over and, overwhelmed by our recently acquired goodies, we patiently stood in line for the rest of the day simply to get a quick clean-up and a painful cold water shave and, although we scarcely finished up smelling of roses, it was, after all, well worth the effort.

Awakened at some God-forsaken hour the following morning, we were, by means of sign language, given to understand that a coal train brought in the previous evening was awaiting unloading in a nearby siding. By gestures and a few unintelligible words of English, we were not at all surprised to learn that we had 'volunteered' to unload this coal train but, and this was the carrot, once it had been emptied, we were to be transported in the empty wagons to Karlsbad where the Americans would be waiting to collect us.

So far so good, we thought, and set to with a will despite the absence of even the crudest tools. However, in a matter of a few hours, exhausted but satisfied, we climbed aboard the empty wagons. Hard luck you could have called it. We sat and waited for the remainder of that day and long into the night, no engine came to connect up to the wagons and towards a freezingly cold dawn, we were off-loaded and, stiff-limbed, returned to the place from whence we had come.

It was only natural that after fitfully dozing, sitting huddled closely together throughout a cold, uncharitable night, tempers were very frayed and brittle the following day. A deputation had approached the Russians hoping to learn what other acts of calculated enlightenment they might or might not have up their sleeves but speaking English to Russians who don't understand English was by its very nature an awfully frustrating situation.

Talk about bringing back hanging, the Russians we met were as thick and uncooperative as a bunch of left wing militants on a picket line. Attempting to alleviate the tension, one of their ilk must have spread it round that the German word 'Bald' might well be understood if it were repeated often enough. In their thinking, they were for once perfectly correct as in the past, whenever the Germans were approached by us with a demand for something or other one of their two stock answers was brought into play. The first and possibly the more abused of the two was, 'Es Gibts Kein' literally translated as meaning 'We've got bugger all!' The other word, 'Bald', now even more frequently brought into play as a Russian master stroke simply meant 'soon' and with their nonsensical power of reasoning, the Russians obviously felt that they had now overcome the anxiety that was apparently plaguing the English. Yes, we most certainly had experienced throughout our period of captivity the full impact of 'Bald', the Teutonic equivalent of the Spanish mañana – 'Soon'.

Later that same day a further ripple of optimism echoed around the camp. Another coal train had arrived and, or so it was said, when we had unloaded this one we would most assuredly be on our way to Karlsbad. Being more or less trapped in a 'good hiding to nothing situation', we set out to unload these Czechoslovakian black diamonds although understandably with little of the same euphoric degree of enthusiasm which had encouraged us to unload the first train. Was this, we wondered, to become a repetition of the last fiasco? We were reluctant to consider what might happen should this prove to be yet another let down. The general feeling of optimism created by our recent meeting with the Swiss and the promise of an early transfer to the Americans was beginning to dissipate and was at that moment in danger of being replaced with a feeling of frustration, desperation and depression.

We had once more, but with a great deal of effort, successfully completed the unloading of the coal almost bare-handed apart from the positively useless addition of a few, believe it or not, garden forks. We again took up our positions on board the wagons and sat not too patiently to await the next move. Daylight slowly turned to twilight and even more slowly still to a saturating blanket of darkness. Aggravated by a nagging feeling of uncertainty, petty bickering and even the odd fight was starting to disrupt what had earlier been, under the circumstances, a bunch of very reasonable but very weary optimists.

Almost on the point of dozing off, I was conscious of a strange jerking movement and, most likely dulled by a nearness to sleep, we were, as can well be appreciated, delighted to hear the sound of cheering and excited shouting whilst at the same time Jock confirmed that we had at last got an engine which by all accounts was now coupled up to our train.

Shortly afterwards and after a few false starts and a lot of intermittent jerking we set off with a final shrill shriek of the engine's whistle. Little point now, we all thought, in maintaining our anxious vigil. We were on the move, a move which would take us along to the American Sector and from there back to our homes. Mentally and physically exhausted, we fell back in our corners and slept our way through to Karlsbad.

Dawn in Karlsbad was not a terribly appealing picture I might add. We hastily and unceremoniously unloaded ourselves on the deserted station platform where we were left, stupified by sleep and the cold, to work out our next move. The town itself, or what we could see of it, appeared to have been very badly damaged but whether that was on account of shelling or from air attacks was a matter on which we were unable to decide.

What we did know was that we'd been dumped here and that there was no American reception committee. We also knew that we had not eaten since goodness knows when and the thought of chewing anything edible and washing it down with anything drinkable was a thought too tantalizing to dwell upon.

Jock and I decided to break off from the main party and circulate in the hope of finding something worth eating and, having walked only a short distance, we were startled to see an old man emerge from the ruins of a nearby pile of bricks that had once been a home. Jock, the eternal optimist, called out to the man asking in German if he had any food and on receiving a rather non-committal reply decided to press still further for an answer. After a more prolonged conversation, a noticeable change became apparent in the man's attitude: he had at last realised that we were English and not the Russians he had feared we might be. With his natural aptitude for foraging, Jock took full charge of the proceedings and, putting me in the picture, he explained that the man and his wife, both Südeten Germans, lived in the rubble which he said, pointing to it, was all that was left of their home. They had, for the past week or so managed to eke out a frugal existence living in a cellar under the rubble.

Inviting us to go back with him to meet his wife, we managed to claw our way through the rubble simply by slipping and sliding down an almost unnegotiable path until we finally came to rest several feet below ground outside a makeshift door. Passing through into their living room we were surprised to witness the full extent of this old couple's adaptability. The room contained, in the main, a large double bed, although how on earth they had managed to manipulate this solid, cumbersome item of furniture down to the cellar and through the entrance which we had so hazardously negotiated remains to this day a complete enigma. They had two armchairs, also solid and heavy, and both incongruously sporting a pure white and artisitically embroidered chair back. There was a profusion of pictures adorning the walls, a copious assortment of bric-a-brac, an ornate brass oil lamp and a wash bowl complete with a matching floral water jug. This temporary sanctuary had obviously been created with great care and lots of scavenging, but what most took our attention was the primus-type stove situated on a box in the far corner of the cellar with, heaped alongside, a mouth-watering selection of vegetables.

The old woman, observing the focus of our attention, offered us the full use of their bed and promised that whilst we rested, she would prepare for us a thick vegetable soup. In the meantime the old man had agreed to keep a careful watch on the railway station and, at the first sign of any American transport, he would come back and warn us.

Fully clothed and lousy, we spread out on the bed and almost instantly fell into a deep sleep. It seemed no time at all before we were awakened by the old woman who, proudly pointing to her stew pot, proclaimed the meal as being ready to eat. I still don't know whether my taste had been irreparably changed by hunger or whether, in fact, this woman had actually produced a miracle from the proceeds of a few vegetables but, either way, it was absolutely delicious. Enjoying this bountiful offering required maximum concentration on our part and, just on the point of accepting the woman's offer to partake of a second helping, in came the old man gasping for breath having over-exerted himself in his effort to get back as quickly as possible to let us know that a convoy of American trucks were parked by the railway station with their crews. Some were loading aboard those ex-prisoners who had stayed put, whilst others were out scouring the immediate area for stragglers such as ourselves.

Delighted to hear the news we bid a hasty farewell to our benefactors and, complete with stamp album and an uncomfortably overloaded stomach, we made tracks for the station. Our first glimpse of these free Americans brought a lump to our throats. We'd covered hundreds of miles under, I'd say, quite spartan conditions to get this far. I thought of Jack now lying in some remote and uncared-for grave along with many others and remembered that here we were on possibly one of the last stages of our return home, and he in his final resting place, a mere six or perhaps seven weeks short of survival.

The welcome, however, of our American Allies scarcely came up to our expectations. We were unceremoniously ordered to climb aboard the trucks without assistance although being fair, a set of wooden steps had been placed by the tailboard of each truck so that we could more easily clamber our way inside. Our liberators, short on speech but excitable in their actions were all noticeably wearing protective gloves and face masks. I don't know what diseases they suspected we were plagued with but, my God, they weren't going to allow us to push any of it their way.

Answering our clamorous calls for information, a response to the effect that we were to be taken to an airfield near Pilsen was enough to prompt a loud and prolonged cheer from all present, and sure enough, within a matter of two hours we were driven through the main gates of a recently-liberated airfield.

Escorted by a team of motor cycle outriders we were summarily despatched to an isolated patch sheltered by a small copse of pine trees on the fringe of the airfield and alighted to find ourselves in the middle of a not-too-welcoming committee of white-coated, gloved, masked and rubber-booted medical staff. In ordinary service life we had always looked upon the American serviceman as easy-going, sometimes loud and frequently over-generous, but their behaviour here bordered on uncontrollable paranoia. We were abruptly and without ceremony ordered to strip and place ourselves arms and legs spread-eagled on the ground and, having carried out this instruction, we were then individually assailed from all sides by an over-indulgent team of medical orderlies impressively (if that is the word for it) equipped with outsize spray guns and apparently committed to waging total war on our lice-infested bodies. No area was sacred, we rolled over back and then front on their instructions. Heads were the subject of an extra savage onslaught, armpits, chest, crotch and a final good luck burst spitefully directed at our heads. Surprised yes – indeed we were – but witnessing the incongruous sight of a group of white powder-coated skeletal-like characters such as we were, we could only roll about literally aching with peals of uncontrollable laughter.

Sobering up and coming to grips with the situation, we did, after all, have perfectly valid grounds for resenting the manner of our reception and we immediately went into the attack demanding food and drink. This was promised and within a reasonably short period of time, trestle tables were set up and shortly afterwards a small convoy of light vehicles descended on us, this time bearing an enormous supply of small cans of meat and vegetables, an unlimited supply of cigarettes, small individual methylated spirit stoves for heating our food and packets of coffee powder.

The gentle warning, 'everything has a price', could, we reminded ourselves, scarcely go unheeded as the self-same medical team as of late alighted from the bowels of the leading truck: no food until we again strip off, lie down etc. etc. Grumbling, but finding this one of the so many offers we had been unable to refuse, we obliged by again sporting our persons in an attitude of total submission on the ground.

This aggravating exercise again successfully carried out temporarily released us from any further obligations and, with a whoop of greedy delight we took a swift dive towards the tempting array of still more tinned food. But added frustration was to follow, indeed the same pattern was to unfold itself each meal time for the remainder of our stay as, in an anxious voice almost trembling with subdued hysteria, we were warned not to approach the food table until the group of orderlies, lacking the protective clothing of the medical team, had safely withdrawn beyond any possible physical contact with our party.

Containers of water had been brought along for our use along with a box of small but useful can openers which were to prove indispensable, as were the small spirit stoves, although due to necessity, we had to eat the contents of the M. and V. cans in order to fill those same cans with water for coffee making.

It seemed an endless procedure but we didn't mind. We ate the food cold and straight from the can and then smoked and smoked Camels, Phillip Morris and Chesterfields by the score whilst we waited blissfully anticipating the pleasurable luxury of a brew of real coffee. Towards dusk, and with the threat of yet another cold night approaching, we nominated a delegation to negotiate with the Americans for a supply of blankets. Panic stations were quick to follow as the Yanks, keeping a constant eye on our movements from the distant security of their side of the airfield, became both alarmed and agitated to see this ragged group of lice-infested invaders apparently hell bent on pentrating their secure, germ free citadel.

Coming out to meet our delegation which by this time had ground to a halt, the Yanks, insistent on maintaining a respectable distance between themselves and our party, readily conceded to our latest demand and agreed to supply us with a reasonable quantity of blankets providing our negotiators returned to join the main party. This promise was given and within a short period of time we were comfortably propped up with many camp fires blazing, a plentiful supply of cigarettes and coffee and – wait for it – one real woollen blanket per man.

On the following day, which again turned out to be pleasantly warm and sunny, we sat and sunned ourselves. Blissfully observing life from our remote corner of isolation we lazily plotted the frequent movement of aircraft in and out of the airfield. The main type of transport seemed to be the

C47 Dakota used as a workhorse throughout the war as an all-purpose troop or cargo carrying aircraft. How long, we wondered, were we likely to be here before being flown out in one? Boredom, born out of sheer inactivity, was rapidly becoming our main enemy. We were deloused, we ate and we slept but we still got restless. However, one particular highlight had resulted in sending our pulse rate up a notch or two – we had each been allocated an embarkation number and, or so we were informed, when our number was called out we were to proceed to the perimeter track and await boarding a C47 which would taxi over to our section of the airfield. I've long since forgotten my number but at that particular time it was firmly fixed in my mind.

Restless and totally inactive, we were slowly becoming more stimulated both physically and mentally by the satisfactory albeit monotonous diet of canned meat and veg. Our horizons were overdue for a period of enlightenment and, I suppose, for the sheer hell of it, we decided that after dark we would do a spot of what we called 'panhandling'. Don't quite know where the term originated but I do know what it meant 'scrounging' and, on a suitably dark night, we set out to invade the forbidden territory.

Being seasoned veterans although admittedly perhaps a trifle rusty, we surreptitiously circled our way around the outer perimeter of the airfield heading in the general direction of the main administration block. We knew that the guards patrolling the airfield were armed and, being a trifle jumpy might not hesitate before firing, and so you can imagine our chuckles of satisfaction at by-passing several not-so-very-alert and unsuspecting protectors of U.S. property.

Arriving spot-on at our predetermined target we were able to move about in the enveloping darkness completely unchallenged, even though on occasion we actually passed almost shoulder to shoulder with several more American Servicemen who remained completely unaware of our presence. One building more brightly lit for some reason or other gave us a clue that it could be either the cookhouse or the canteen and, striking it lucky, we were able at our first attempt to locate the cookhouse. All these buildings were of concrete construction and most likely built by the Germans shortly after annexing the territory back in 1938. Finding our way between the refuse bins, we quickly discovered a basement stockroom with an outside door at the bottom of a few steps secured with an antiquated and fragile padlock. In a matter of seconds the four of us were inside fumbling our way along the shelves hopefully selecting for ourselves a more interesting and varied supply of goodies more likely to titillate our jaded taste buds. With a gasp of surprise someone muttered that in his neck of the woods, he'd found an assortment of cooking utensils and we, well aware of the fact that from now onwards our aim would be to cook in quantity, quietly decided to liberate two king-size cooking pots.

Gleefully carrying out a quick stock check, we carefully adjusted the remaining stock on the shelves in the hope that our rather savage depletion of the Americans' rations might well remain undetected – some hope!

Our exit, noisy though it turned out to be, was made without attracting any undue attention and perhaps carelessly but rather luckily we returned to our camp site unchallenged.

Unable, on account of the darkness, to examine our loot, we decided in favour of hiding our booty by spacing it out in different parts of the nearby undergrowth and, fully satisfied with the result of our labours, we decided to sleep on it and with visions of canned hot dogs, canned fruit and other such mind-blowing delicacies, we drifted off into a dreamless slumber.

Awakening to a distinct nip in the air and a childlike feeling of anticipation reminiscent to a certain extent, I suppose, of Christmases long since past, incautious and uncaringly concerned as to whether or not our calculated break-in of the previous night would result in a search that might well compromise our early departure from Czechoslovakia, we very quickly retrieved all our spoils from their different hideouts. Imagine our sense of outrage – all the contents were identical and they were all M. and V. Prisoners in war time and, I suppose, prisoners in peace time, due to their very circumstances develop a strain of stoic indifference towards ordinary setbacks which is a quality difficult to describe. I quote as an example our reaction to this disappointing situation. We got our recently-acquired pots, filled one brimful with this now over-familiar meat stew and the other with water. A raging fire lighted under each one was soon merrily crackling away heating a stew and boiling water which no one really wanted.

Sitting by our fires, deep in thought, at first unable to accept as believable a voice repeating over and over again a series of numbers, it slowly began to register that the numbers being called belonged to us. We, us, we were on the way out! Hastily delving into a nearby bush where I had secreted my treasured stamp album which, as I could see it now, was only a stone's throw away from making me a very rich man, I wrapped my blanket around my shoulders and clutching my spoils of war rather than securing it on my back, I moved out towards our embarkation point.

For those unfamiliar with the layout of a C47 let it be said that it has a single rear entrance which is reached by climbing three or possibly four metal steps securely hinged to the bottom of the entrance. Breezily approaching the steps and without a care in the world, I was distinctly alarmed to note that on either side of the aircraft steps stood an American Snowdrop (military policeman), one black and one white. Their orders were soon to become painfully obvious as, bearing in mind the shortage of air transport, weight was an over-riding factor and as such we were summarily ordered to shed all surplus weight which even included our threadbare greatcoats and blankets. Lots of chaps were unhappily surrendering their loot which, in a way, I suppose roughly equated to the price of a ticket home.

For a moment or two as I approached the steps of the aircraft I had a feeling that the bottom was to fall out of my world. This, I thought, was for the very first time in my life, a chance to create a new beginning for myself with the aid of the cash I would hopefully raise from the sale of my cherished stamp album, but at that moment in time I realised my dream was rapidly evaporating. Pausing for a brief second long enough only to catch a fleeting glimpse of the over-riding greed in the black American's eye, I placed my sacrificial offering fairly and squarely into his outstretched arms whilst at the same time muttering to him, 'Here, Yank, buy yourself a Hershey Bar.'

EPILOGUE

The beginning of a new life was taking place even as the C47 flew gracefully albeit noisily above the so recently fought over cities, towns and countryside of Germany, en route for England.

Little wonder perhaps that our feelings were so mixed as to conjure up a sense of anxiety in respect of what the future might hold. For good or evil we were rapidly being drawn away from everything that had happened, a past which had produced a balanced mixture of saints and sinners, a past which so recently had left a friend lying in an alien grave near Bautzen and a disturbing overpowering sense of fear for a world whose weaknesses were even now being probed by our former unpredictable ally, Soviet Russia, whose hordes we had so recently seen pillaging and desecrating the soil of a crippled Czechoslovakia.

In the years that followed, I have learned that Jack Pedersen's remains, after prolonged negotiations with the eastern bloc authorities, were removed to the British and Commonwealth 1939–1945 War Cemetery in the Charlottenburg district of Berlin almost three years after the war ended. Lofty Banks, my friend from Lamsdorf and Klimontow sadly died of a brain tumour a few years ago and Dick Howarth is buried in the War Cemetery in Anzio. Jock (or Alec), my Scottish friend, has regrettably disappeared without trace even though I have attempted by various means to trace his whereabouts. Ben, Ron and Jeff sadly remain unaccounted for as do the Royal Marines who so generously and unselfishly helped me during my times of stress in the farm at Drauskowitz near Bautzen.

Possibly and through the hoped-for circulation of this book, some thread, broken so long ago, may well become complete after all, who knows?

The cookhouse Feldwebel from Dulag 339 at Mantova who contrived so diligently to make the lives of the inmates of that camp a complete misery failed to survive for long. I hear on good authority that his demise took place dramatically and quickly when the camp was straffed by the Americans some time in the summer of 1944. Our Feldwebel in charge at Klimontow was also despatched in early 1945 whilst conducting a party of prisoners on a forced march through Poland and Germany. He was shot and killed during a surprise air raid carried out by the Russians straffing the roads.